sound the trumpet!

MESSAGES to

EMPOWER african american men

sound the trumpet!

MESSAGES to

EMPOWER african american men

edited by darryl d. sims

Judson Press • Valley Forge

sound the trumpet!

MESSAGES to EMPOWER african american men

Judson Press has made every effort to trace the ownership of all quotes.
In the event of a question arising from the use of a quote, we regret any
error made and will be pleased to make the necessary correction
in future printings and editions of this book.

Bible quotations in this volume are from *The Holy Bible*, King James
Version (KJV); and from the New Revised Standard Version of the Bible,
copyright © 1989 by the Division of Christian Education of the National
Council of the Churches of Christ in the United States of America. Used by
permission. All rights reserved. (NRSV)

Library of Congress Cataloging-in-Publication Data

Sound the trumpet! : messages to empower African American men / edited
by Darryl D. Sims.
       p. cm.
ISBN 0-8170-1437-3 (pbk. : alk. paper)
1. African American men—Religious life. 2. African American men—
Conduct of life. 3. Sermons, American—African American authors.
I. Sims, Darryl D.

BL625.2 .S68 2003
248.8'42'08996073—dc21   20020209858

Printed in the U.S.A.

08 07 06 05 04 03 02

10 9 8 7 6 5 4 3 2 1

contents

foreword

in the past few years, a number of people have seen the need for an anthology of sermons that would focus on the plight of African American men in the United States of America. The problem has become all the more alarming as one notes the dramatic increase in the rate of incarcerated black men in America compared with the relative paucity of them who attend church regularly. Many local churches are beginning to give greater attention to the complex issues that contribute to the destabilization of black men in America through men's retreats, regional or ecumenical men's conferences, and national confabs for African American men. However, few of these efforts have produced a body of literature that identifies and analyzes specific aspects of the social pathology plaguing black men in America today, while also outlining a spiritual remedy from a contemporary Christian perspective. With the publication of *Sound the Trumpet*, we have evidence that some "brothers" exist who sincerely wish to fill this gap.

Darryl D. Sims is one of those rare community activists who has long involved himself in church-based educational and empowerment programs. Throughout his seminary training, I witnessed a process of unusual growth in terms of his synthesizing diverse past experiences—not all of them pleasant—into a creative agenda for social change, beginning with efforts to revitalize the spirituality of African American men. In his church and community work since graduating from Howard University, Darryl has aligned himself with one of the most gifted leaders and preachers in the black church, Rev. Dr. Charles E. Booth of Columbus, Ohio. I count myself fortunate to have been a participant-leader working with both of them in what turned out to be two exciting, spirit-filled regional conferences for black men. This book is a surprising result of those men's conferences inasmuch as they substantiated the critical need for more literature on this topic and provided the inspiration to approach specific individuals as prospective authors for a book.

Sound the Trumpet speaks to one of the most pressing issues that threatens the viability and survival of the black community in America today. Its publication is timely as much attention understandably has shifted to feminist and womanist concerns. This book, however, serves as a necessary reminder that black men still represent in America a kind of "public enemy number one" and are often so treated in the media, political process, criminal justice system, and business world by the majority culture. To change such a woeful circumstance, black men themselves will have to undergo a paradigm shift of the first order. They must stop idle complaining and mindless ego competition, and cease imitating the worst elements in a majority culture of materialism and hoarding.

Instead, this book reintroduces the Bible and its treasure trove of instructive messages and images that could assist black men— who are often stereotyped and the subject of caricature by society —to take themselves and their spirituality more seriously as they allow themselves to be transformed, rather than merely comprising a set of social problems on the periphery of American society. Thus, this book is a welcomed warning and a challenge; the latter, if accepted, with God's help could assist a group that has been so long neglected to rise to its feet and save even the soul of a nation too willing to risk greatness for warring madness.

The editor, Darryl Sims, frames the entries in this collection of sermons with his provocative opening entitled "State of Emergency" and the closing offering, "The Burden Bearer." Between these two bookends stand sobering, insightful, and yet uplifting biblical themes that are pressed into service in order to get the attention of many of the African American men who believe that we are not interested in their special circumstances. Readers will delight in studying the rhetorical and interpretive skills found in the contributors who, for the most part, are widely recognized as prophetic voices sounding the trumpet for a people to become better Christian soldiers!

Cain Hope Felder

Howard University, School of Divinity

October 2002

preface

the idea for this book began in 2000 while i was serving as minister of men and evangelism at Mt. Olivet Baptist Church in Columbus, Ohio. As I worked with black men of various ages—from twelve years old to eighty years old—I noticed a commonality among them: So many—too many—of them felt isolated in their pain. Unfortunately, too many were uncomfortable sharing their pain; too many looked at self-exploration and self-disclosure as "unmanly" or as a sign of weakness.

On many occasions, the men would want to meet with me individually after our Friday night men's meeting to discuss pains that they were uncomfortable sharing in a group setting. Each man talked about his feelings of inadequacy as a husband, father, friend, son, mate, and employee. Each was frustrated with and confused about these feelings of inadequacy and expected me, in my role, to say something to help him to hold on for another week. Oftentimes, helping these men was just a matter of my sharing with them a personal testimony or some passage from the Bible to give them hope. These conversations gave them inspiration and began to convince them that they had a destiny to fulfill, despite their feelings of inadequacy, pain, and confusion.

Beyond these meetings, one has only to look at statistics and data on the spiritual, social, economic, and educational lives of African American males to realize that we are not faring well in these realms of life. Compared to black women, fewer black men are attending church. Compared to black women, more black men are socially disadvantaged—more are incarcerated, more are addicted to drugs, more are underemployed and unemployed. Compared to black women, fewer black men are graduating from high school and college. And, frankly, compared to white men and women, black men are faring even worse. Thus, we must raise the question "Why?"

These findings and my encounters with black men have convinced me of one thing: Many African American men have spiritual scar tissue that needs mending. For several years, a question has constantly nagged me: Why do so many black men turn to alcohol, drugs, crime, and sexual misconduct as a way of coping with the issues in their lives? I realized the answer is this: We turn to these behaviors, these outlets, when there is no sustained ministry of some kind in our lives to help us to deal effectively with our issues, concerns, fears, and insecurities.

I have found that we—black men—have within us an innate spiritual presence that, once activated, can usher us into another realm of existence. But to my dismay, I was unable to find a central literary resource that would allow me to reactivate myself and other black men. Nor could I find a book of inspirational sermons designed specifically for the issues that plague black men in America. I had a lot of tapes to help me, but not a lot of literature. Occasionally, I could find a chapter in a book on one or two of these issues, but not a comprehensive book. I could find a book of inspirational sermons from one author, but not a book that was comprised of multiple authors, thereby providing me with a well-rounded view of Jesus the Christ.

Thus, my initial question moved from the aforementioned "Why?" to "Where can African American men turn for a source or resource that helps them to cope effectively with issues in their lives from a spiritual perspective?" The most obvious book is the Bible, the most obvious place is the church, and the most obvious person is a pastor. In addition, black men can now turn to a work of literature that provides answers to these troubling issues. This book of inspirational sermons is intended to be a source and resource that black men can turn to in their daily Christian walk.

It is my prayer, as editor, that this book will be used to encourage and empower African American men so that we may be and become all of what God intends for us to be and to become. Being and becoming are accomplished primarily by realizing that the God of Abraham, Isaac, and Jacob is also *our* God. Jesus the Christ is *our* lifted savior. The Holy Ghost is *our* comforter.

In writing this book, I had several goals in mind. First, I had deliberately chosen to compile an edited book, thus allowing readers access to many voices and viewpoints. Second, the book is contemporary, in that it addresses issues facing black men today, issues facing black men in the realness and rawness of their situation. Third, the book offers a collection of sermons, going beyond providing readers with only devotions and Scriptures. And finally, the book focuses specifically on *black males;* it goes beyond a focus on blacks in general and it goes beyond a focus on males in general. It focuses on both groups—men who are African American.

Given my long-term concerns about the quality of life of African American men, I recently founded Evangucation Ministries, Inc., and DLR Learning Center. Essentially, Evangucation Ministries is a faith-based organization that works with educational institutions and social institutions (e.g., prisons, shelters, etc.) to improve the spiritual, social, psychological, and educational lives of African Americans. DLR Learning Center has more of an educational focus. In this capacity, I attempt to challenge and alter the paradigm of what ought to be taught to and learned by black males. I focus on improving their academic achievement via multicultural education, tutoring, test-taking skills, conflict resolution, anger management, and family involvement, to name a few of the strategies. In their own ways, both organizations attempt to instill hope, identity, and purpose in African American males. And such is the purpose of this collection of sermons.

acknowledgments

writing a book, especially one that focuses on developing individuals spiritually, is a major undertaking. Along the road, one must seek the guidance and support of others in an attempt to present the best of what one has to offer. We all travel many journeys on the road to Christ, and those whose paths we have crossed must forever be given thanks and appreciation. With this in mind, first and foremost, I give thanks to God for this revelation. Second, I give thanks to Dr. Charles E. Booth for allowing me to serve in the dual capacity of Minister of Men and Minister of Evangelism. Third, I give special thanks to Dean Clarence G. Newsome for allowing me to serve as his graduate assistant while at the Howard University School of Divinity. I also give special thanks to Dr. Cain Hope Felder, also of Howard, who served as my mentor and role model. Let me also give thanks to Dr. H. Beecher Hicks Jr., senior pastor of Metropolitan Baptist Church, Washington, D.C., who taught me to always be resourceful and mindful of the role of the minister inside and outside of the church. Finally, I must acknowledge my father, Stanford Sims II, who served many years as a deacon in the church and who taught me the value of worshipping God in truth and in spirit. In their own ways, all of these men have helped me to live, serve, and learn by the Scripture, "And as they came out, they found a man of Cyrene, Simon by name: him they compelled to bear his cross" (Matthew 27:32, KJV).

While all these men and many other persons unnamed in these pages have contributed to my development as a Christian man, there is a rose among the thorns. Men can develop a man in so many ways, but the love of a mother is matchless. It was my mother who prepared me for the ministry of Jesus the Christ.

This book, therefore, is dedicated to the woman, the rose, who raised seven children in the projects by herself (and with God). On behalf of Benita, myself, Marie, Johnny, Tarina, Karen, and LeAnthony: Thank you, Mommy.

In addition, I send all of my love to my daughters, Darnisha, Latecia, and Riele.

And finally, I would be remiss and out of place if I didn't acknowledge the herculean efforts of Donna Y. Ford, Ph.D. She helped me a great deal with the editing of this book.

introduction

a state of EMERGENCY

Then took they Jeremiah, and cast him into the dungeon
of Malchiah the son of Hammelech, that was in the court
of the prison: and they let down Jeremiah with cords. And
in the dungeon there was no water, but mire: so Jeremiah
sunk in the mire. Now when Ebedmelech the Ethiopian,
one of the eunuchs which was in the king's house, heard
that they had put Jeremiah in the dungeon; the king then
sitting in the gate of Benjamin; Ebedmelech went forth
out of the king's house, and spake to the king, saying, My
lord the king, these men have done evil in all that they
have done to Jeremiah the prophet, whom they have cast
into the dungeon; and he is like to die for hunger in the
place where he is: for there is no more bread in the city.
Then the king commanded Ebedmelech the Ethiopian, saying, Take from hence thirty men with thee, and take up
Jeremiah the prophet out of the dungeon, before he die.
(Jeremiah 38:6–10, KJV)

∞

my brothers in christ, we live in a society where
crime, death, moral decay, lack of integrity, lack of respect for dif-
ferences, and little fear of God appear to be the norm. It is no
wonder our country is in the state that it is in. Without a sense of
brotherhood (and sisterhood) among the people of this country,
a future state of emergency is a forgone conclusion. As long as the
chief concern of the rich people is to stay rich, but not to share
their bounty with the least of them, our country will stay divisive
with turmoil and strife. Because those with power are obsessed

with staying in power rather than sharing their power and influence with and for the good of other people, our country is headed toward a time of disaster. As long as the informed are purposeful in keeping many of the marginalized uninformed and misinformed, this country is headed for an implosion—an explosion from within!

America considers 9-11 to be its state of emergency, but I tell you that we, as African Americans, have been in a state of emergency since 1619 when the first twenty slaves were brought to Virginia on a slave ship. We were in a state of emergency in 1863 when the Emancipation Proclamation was signed. During the Jim Crow era, black America was in a state of emergency. During the Vietnam War, black America was in a state of emergency. During the Civil Rights era, black America was in a state of emergency. My brothers, through the Nixon, Reagan, Clinton, and Bush years, black America continues to be in a state of emergency.

Too many social ills of our society have gone unattended for too long. It is only a matter of time before the "have-nots" confront the "haves" in a manner that will produce casualties of a serious kind. Those casualties already represent a state of emergency in America.

Our country, with all of its technology and genius, has chosen to ignore the needs of a huge segment of its population. America has elected to perpetuate the lie that rests within the parchment of the Constitution of the United States; this lie—one of many—declares that the black man in America is only three-fifths of a human being. This country, with all of its greatness, is still behind the "eight ball" of its own ignorance and self-righteousness. This erroneous view of the value (and subsequent devaluing) of the black man in America has forced too many black men into dungeons—dungeons such as drugs, alcohol, low self-esteem, and poor racial identity. And these dungeons, in turn, have created problems that rest and abide in our homes and community.

Author and scholar Jawanza Kunjufu reminds us that for every day in 2002 in black America:

■ One in every three black males is involved in the penal system; this is a state of emergency!

■ Eighty percent of the students who are in special education classes are black males; this is a state of emergency!

■ For every three black females on college campuses, there is one black male; this is a state of emergency!

■ Black males comprise 13 percent of the population in America, yet they make up 35 percent of drug arrests, 55 percent of drug convictions, 74 percent of drug prisoners, and 50 percent of those on death row; this is a state of emergency!

■ Forty percent of black males in America are illiterate; this is a state of emergency!

And because too many of our men are in dungeons, our children are in a state of emergency as well. When black men are in jeopardy, their families are vulnerable and at risk of being systematically dismantled. According to the Children's Defense Fund, in 2002 every day in black America 24 babies die, 514 babies are born into poverty, 423 babies are born to teenage mothers, and 5,542 students are suspended. The list of issues facing black males and their families seems endless.

Psalm 133:1 says, "Behold, how good and how pleasant it is for brethren to dwell together in unity!" One of the worst things that has happened to us as a people and as a church body is the spirit of disharmony that has invaded our sense of oneness. The Bible says that, as long as two or three agree in God's name and are of one accord, then God will be in the midst of all their comings and goings (Matthew 18:19–20). We know that there is only one body, but many members of the church. The Bible shows us the benefits of men working in unity with God, and the benefits of working in unity with each other. Look at what happened when David and Jonathan worked in unity. Look at what happened when Paul and Timothy worked in harmony. Look at what happened when Jesus and Peter were close allies. And, of course, look at what happened when Jesus and John the Baptist worked in unity. Because black men aren't working in unity, other ethnic groups—and women—are surpassing us in all categories.

Therefore, African American brothers are in a state of emergency! Too many of us have given up, fallen into the dungeons of today, and don't know how to climb out. Some of us are in the dungeon of drugs, others are in the dungeon of lust, some are in the dungeon of crime and violence, and others are in the dungeon of self-pity and spiritual apathy, having lost faith in God. Still other African American men are in the dungeon of ignorance, lacking an education or being miseducated in American schools and universities.

African Americans, especially men, are in a state of emergency! It is an unfortunate reality that we are partly responsible for our condition. Too many African American men, young and old, have come to believe the stereotypes placed on black men, that we are shiftless, lazy, irresponsible, lustful, and angry, to name a few things. And too many of our brothers have lived down to those expectations, some even intentionally perpetuating those stereotypes.

Society, with its innumerable social injustices, is also partly responsible. And society's portion of the responsibility is significant. Racism runs rampant in America's workforce, schools, and society at large. Desegregation continues in many schools. Urban schools are underfunded and understaffed. Blacks are often underemployed and underpaid, and the list of injustices goes on.

But there is hope. Just as a black man named Ebedmelech the Ethiopian engineered a plan to save Jeremiah, black men in America must do the same with the help of God. As the sermons in this book espouse, black men must understand the many dungeons in their own lives and in the lives of their fellow African

Americans. In addition to such understanding, we must find answers that rest within ourselves, within our own powers. We must begin to take control of our lives, our emotions, our actions, and our spirituality. But how?

Looking inward to find answers and ways to change our lives is a step in the right direction. But the ultimate understanding and the ultimate answers rest with knowing and living by God's Word. Each essay in this book has a different message. Each man in the essay has a different story to tell. But each essay and each man has one answer, one place where they turn—to God the Father, God the Son, and God the Holy Ghost—to move from a state of emergency to a state of grace.

This book is an attempt to sound the trumpet of what "thus says the Lord." I have sought the assistance of some of the greatest gospel trumpeters in the world. Many times, priests were required to blow trumpets before battle: "You shall march around the city seven times, and the priests shall blow the trumpets. It shall come to pass, when they make a long blast with the ram's horn, and when you hear the sound of the trumpet, that all the people shall shout with a great shout; then the wall of the city will fall down flat. And the people shall go up every man straight before him" (Joshua 6:5–6, NKJV).

Before, during, and after a battle, trumpets were used to send instructions to the men who were engaged in a state of emergency. But the trumpets were also used to assemble the leaders of a congregation—and indeed, the entire village. The trumpets made a distinctive and alarming sound. The priests, prophets, and preachers in the African American community will have to continue to make such distinctive and alarming sounds through their proclamations that God specializes in coming through for his people in times of trouble. Sound the trumpet, so that all men, women, and children of God will know that God can lift them up and carry them through all their emergencies. Sound the trumpet of God! Sound the trumpet!

chapter one

a BLACK MAN in a bad situation

charles e. booth

They compelled a passer-by, who was coming in from the country, to carry his cross; it was Simon of Cyrene, the father of Alexander and Rufus. (Mark 15:21, NRSV)

∞

not long ago, hbo brought to the television screen the epic real-life drama *Boycott*, which told the story of the 365-day bus boycott in Montgomery, Alabama, initiated by Mrs. Rosa Parks, who refused to yield her seat to a white man. It was this event that catapulted Dr. Martin Luther King Jr. to national and international prominence.

Much has happened since that episode in our history, and tremendous strides have been made in the area of race relations. The United States Supreme Court, for example, struck down segregation in public transportation facilities in 1956. The higher court wrote a similar decision in 1963, declaring segregation to be unconstitutional in restaurants and hotel facilities. The Civil Rights Act was passed in 1964, the Voting Rights Act in 1965, and Open Housing legislation in 1966. We have seen two black men occupy seats on the Supreme Court. Barbara Jordan became the first African American to address the Democratic National Convention on July 12, 1976. Today, in the George W. Bush administration, we have an African American secretary of state—Colin Powell; an African American national security advisor—Condoleeza Rice; and an African American secretary of education—Ron Paige. Indeed, no one can deny that significant

and monumental strides have been made in the area of race relations in this country.

We have come a long way, but I believe that we still have a long
way to go. For instance, there exists an insidious display of racism
today known as "racial profiling." It is particularly operative in
our cities, suburbs, and along our highways. where law enforce-
ment officers stop, at will, African Americans and other racially
diverse persons who drive upscale automobiles and dress well.
These persons are stopped not because they have done anything
wrong, nor because they have broken any law. These persons are
stopped simply because of the pigmentation of their skin. Mark
15:21 reveals to us that racial profiling isn't something new.

It is Passover season in our text. Jews have come from all over
the then-known world to Jerusalem to celebrate this sacred feast,
which commemorates the deliverance of the Jews from Egypt on
that night when the death angel made his midnight ride through
Egypt and destroyed the first-born males of every home on which
the blood of the Paschal lamb was not sprinkled. According to
the Gospel of Mark, one such visitor to Jerusalem that day was
a man from North Africa, Simon of Cyrene. Colonies of Jews
existed outside of Judah, and this man, Simon, hailed from a
place that is today known as Libya. Every God-fearing Jew
desired to celebrate the Passover in Jerusalem—the city of
David—at least once in his or her lifetime. In all probability,
Simon had been saving all of his life so that he might make such
a pilgrimage and fulfill his dream.

One must remember that, at this time in history, Palestine was
an occupied territory; therefore, any man might be "impressed"
into Roman service for any task. There were no questions to be
asked and no dialogue was to follow. A Roman centurion could
demand, or impress, whomever he chose into service to perform
a task. The sign of impressment was a tap on the shoulder with
the flat of a Roman spear.

So here is Simon from Cyrene, a black man from North Africa, minding his own business. He has come all the way from northern Africa to attend the Passover feast in Jerusalem and, suddenly, he is impressed into service. A Nazarene carpenter named Jesus has just been indicted in the Praetorium at the behest of the crowd and must suffer death by crucifixion. The longest possible route was always taken to the place of crucifixion, with the indicted criminal carrying his own cross, and a Roman soldier walking in front with a sign indicating the crime committed by the guilty one. It was this sign that would be nailed above the head of the criminal as he hung upon his cross. The longest route was always taken so that the majority of people would be able to see the accused, read the sign bearing his crime, and thus be struck with fear so that they would think before committing such a crime themselves.

Jesus, weak from all that he has had to endure with regard to sleeping disciples, betrayal, denial, kangaroo courts, and the will of a mob, stumbles and falls beneath the weight of the cross he is made to bear. It is at this point that Simon of Cyrene receives that dreaded tap on the shoulder from the flat of a Roman spear and is thus impressed into helping Jesus carry his cross.

Out of all the people watching Jesus carry his cross, why was Simon singled out? It could be that he happened to be closest to Jesus or the centurion who impressed him. Obviously, he was at the wrong place at the wrong time! I am convinced that Simon was made to carry that cross because he was a black man and a Jew. His skin color was immediately in the mind of the Roman soldier. Simon was a victim of racial profiling. He had to do what the Roman soldier demanded because he was in occupied territory and his skin color was the badge of his inferiority and servitude.

Even today, our blackness is a badge to others. Do you want to know why black men are followed at the grocery store and at the mall? It is because of labels that have been applied to us by others. Here in the text we have a black man in a bad situation. How did Simon handle this situation, and what are the implications for us as African American men?

The first thing the text says is that Simon was compelled or forced to carry the cross of the Christ. Herein is a great and fundamental lesson of life, my fellow black men. There are certain things in life over which we have no control and we are compelled to do them. There are some things we must do because there are no options. We are compelled to learn how to walk, regardless of how many times we fall. We are compelled to honor and love our parents, regardless of their imperfections. We are compelled to love our neighbor as we love ourselves, regardless of the possible unfairness. We are compelled to study and learn in order to realize our potential, and to develop our gifts, regardless of the quality of our educational establishments. We are compelled to recognize that, while God is good, life is not always fair. We are compelled to realize that in this life we will always have trials, troubles, tribulations, and temptations, regardless of how much we pray. We are compelled to realize that "Rome was not built in a day" and that patience is a virtue to be learned, regardless of how badly we want something.

Even though Simon did not want to carry the cross of Jesus, he recognized that, given that set of particular circumstances, he had no option or alternative in the matter. My brothers, as fathers, we have failed to teach this generation that they have very few options in their youth. We have substituted mandates with options. During my youth, mandates were clearly defined. We were compelled or forced to see an education as the necessary vehicle for getting ahead. We were compelled or forced to honor and respect our elders. We were compelled or forced never to talk back to our elders. We were compelled or forced to open doors and pull out chairs for young ladies. We were compelled or forced to go to church, to go to Sunday school, to do chores, and to bring home good grades. Words such as *options* and *alternatives* were alien to my vocabulary when it came to the rules and regulations of my youth.

On the night of July 9, 1893, James Cornish was rushed to the hospital with a stab wound to his heart. He had been taken to the emergency room in Provident Hospital, Chicago's first hospital open to all races. The next day, July 10, 1893, Dr. Daniel Hale Williams, Provident's founder, was forced to try a radical procedure that was the only chance to save Cornish's life. With a team of six staff surgeons, Dr. Williams made an incision in Cornish's chest, sutured the artery, then closed the wound in the heart and successfully completed the world's first open heart surgery. Daniel Hale Williams had no options. He was compelled to found a hospital for all people and to save a man's life. Brothers, there will be times in our lives when we, like Daniel Hale Williams and like Simon, will not have options and we must do what we have to do.

Second, we learn from the text that Simon recognized that he had to do whatever was necessary in order to survive. Simon knew that he could not rebel against the Roman guard. The Roman guard had both authority and artillery. It would have been stupid for Simon not to do as he had been instructed. This was not about pride or ego. This was not a test of his manhood. This was about literal survival!

I am convinced that deliberatly Mark makes known the names of Simon's sons—Alexander and Rufus—who go on to become significant in the early church. Simon had sons, and to not do as he was forced might possibly mean that he would die and never see his sons again. He must, therefore, bear the indignity, grit his teeth, and do as he was told by the enemy so that he would live and see his children. Again, black men in bad situations always knew they could make it as long as they had a sense of God in all of their doings. Simon kept his focus on his purpose as a father.

He knew that God would want him to assist in the raising of his children as a responsible father would. Therefore, Simon did what he had to do to survive. We as black men have to do the same. We must think about the next generation and how we can assist them in their preparation.

Charles Darwin contends, in *The Origin of the Species*, that "only the strong survive." We must, my brothers, understand that strength is not always defined in terms of the physical or the anatomical. The greatest strength is often determined and defined by one's ability to make the right decisions and the sanest of choices at the right time. Strength might mean being quiet when you really want to cuss somebody out. Strength, my brothers, might mean walking away from an argument rather than continuing it. Strength might mean speaking up when others around you hold their peace. Trust God to instruct and inform you on when to do the things that will help you to serve and to survive.

African American youth, males in particular, need to understand that we have survived these 383 years because we had to "laugh when we were not tickled and scratch when we did not itch!" We sometimes laugh at the "Steppin' Fetchits" and others we have labeled as "Uncle Toms." However, we must understand that even the "Uncle Toms" were necessary for our survival. African American nationalists frequently berate Booker T. Washington to the exaltation of W. E. B. DuBois. DuBois was the first African American to get a Ph.D. from Harvard, and he authored such works as *The Souls of Black Folk* and "The Talented Tenth" (an essay). He also founded *The Crisis*—the national chronicle of the NAACP. However, while DuBois left us writings, Booker T. Washington left us Tuskegee University.

Survival is never a choice between "either/or." Survival is always about "both/and." In order to survive as Washington and DuBois, Malcolm and King, politics and the church, and the justice system and protests, Simon had enough sense to realize that, if he was going to survive and see his sons, then he would have to carry the cross of this barefoot Nazarene.

Finally, and this is most important, Simon did what he was compelled to do, and thereby fulfilled his reason for coming to Jerusalem—he ended up in the temple celebrating the Passover. His pride was damaged. His ego was bruised. However, Simon fulfilled his purpose for coming to Jerusalem. Look at what possibly occurred:

While in the temple celebrating the Passover—the deliverance of the Jews from Egypt—Simon could well have asked the Lord to deliver him from the pain and the agony of his experience. What better place than the temple and what better time than the Passover to plead to God for deliverance! Deliverance from personal pain. Deliverance from social, political, and economic pain. Simon desired deliverance from his personal pain, and also from the pain of Roman oppression and domination.

While carrying the cross, Simon might well have followed Jesus to Calvary and not only watched Jesus die, but also heard him dying. What could he have heard? "Father, forgive them; for they do not know what they are doing" (Luke 23:34). "It is finished" (John 19:30). "Father, into your hands I commend my spirit" (Luke 23:46).

Simon went back to Cyrene a far different man than when he came. I am convinced that Simon went back home touched, disturbed, and eventually convinced that Jesus is the Christ. My brothers, how, then, do you explain Mark's mentioning of Alexander and Rufus, who go on to be eminent figures in the early church—Alexander in Ephesus and Rufus in Rome? Their daddy's faith became infectious and contagious, so much so that they became convinced of this Christ who died on Calvary but who arose on that third day morning!

There is a lesson to be found here. Regardless of how difficult, dark, discouraging, and disappointing life might be, go to the sanctuary. Brothers, if you are in a bad situation, go to the sanctuary. I believe that Simon did this, and, in so doing, he was able to place in perspective the painful and disjointed realities of his life. He emerged whole, not splintered. He emerged challenged, thoughtful, and energized, not unchallenged, thoughtless, and defeated. He left home with an old faith, but returned home with the rudimentary beginnings of a new faith.

God may put you in what, at that moment, seems like a bad situation, but he has a reason. He can and will turn that bad situation around if you believe in him and live by his word. If he can turn the situation around for Simon, he can turn the situation around for you. God never promised us a smooth sailing; he challenges us with trials and tribulations. In the midst of being in what seems to be a bad situation, we must remain steadfast in our faith. If we trust in God, we can weather the storms; we can grow as African American men, husbands, fathers, and brothers.

The Bible says, "Be strong and bold; have no fear or dread of them, because it is the LORD your God who goes with you; he will not fail you or forsake you" (Deuteronomy 31:6). "A good man falls seven times, but gets back up" (Proverbs 24:16, paraphrase). Jesus said, "He that abideth in me, and I in him, the same bringeth forth much fruit: for without me ye can do nothing" (John 15:5 KJV). "You are from God, and have conquered them; for the one who is in you is greater than the one who is in the world" (1 John 4:4). God saved David, who was in a bad situation. God saved Daniel, who was in a bad situation. God saved three Hebrew boys, who were in a bad situation. Surely, that same God can save you and me from any bad situation.

chapter two
fighting the WRONG enemies
jeremiah a. wright jr.

When he went out the next day, he saw two Hebrews fighting; and he said to the one who was in the wrong, "Why do
you strike your fellow Hebrew?" (Exodus 2:13, NRSV)

∞

at our church's recent men's conference, where
over 400 brothers gathered for a weekend of prayer and study and
worship, one theme was repeated over and over again. This theme
is blood-chilling when you stop to think about it. This predomi-
nant theme was how black men remain the primary target in an
oppressive society that sees black men as a dangerous threat.

Prior to September 11, 2001, when you heard the term "racial
profiling," it was automatically understood that the term referred
to black men. The New Jersey State Police were taken to court
and found guilty of racial profiling for stopping black men on the
state turnpike and on the highways, for looking primarily for
black men driving a Mercedes or Lexus, driving Navigators with
chrome wheels, and wearing earrings and dreads, beards, or dark
glasses. In the minds of the police, these African American men
had to be up to something illegal. The assumption was that they
were either selling dope or using dope. The black man was the
primary target in an oppressive society that sees black men as a
dangerous threat.

There was a story recently in *JET* magazine about a white
police officer who was being harassed by his fellow white officers,
threatened by his fellow officers, and on the verge of losing his

job because he broke the blue code of silence and blew the whistle on the specific instructions his police commander had given the officers in carrying out successful racial profiling. The black man is the primary target in an oppressive society that sees black men as a dangerous threat.

A black Haitian, Abner Louima, was viciously sodomized by white police in New York, Guliani's New York, with a toilet plunger rammed into his rectum by police. Why? Because he was black. Because he was Haitian. He was the primary target in an oppressive society that sees black men as a dangerous threat.

A black African from Guinea, Ahmadou Diallo, was cut to shreds in a hail of forty-one bullets as he reached for his wallet—bullets shot by a bevy of white police in Guliani's New York. Why? Because he was black. He was a primary target in an oppressive society that sees black men as a dangerous threat.

An unarmed, nineteen-year-old black male, Timothy Thomas, was gunned down by a white cop, Steve Roach, in Cincinnati, Ohio, and the white cop was let go by a white judge who saw the murder as justifiable. How was it justifiable? Because the black boy was the primary target in an oppressive society that sees black men, regardless of their age, as a dangerous threat.

I am in the text. Come with me to the Word of God and hear the same old story in a different key. One day, after Moses had grown up, he went out to his people and saw their forced labor. That is slavery. That is oppression, in case you missed it. In Exodus 1:8–10, a new king arose over Egypt who said to his people, "Come, let us deal shrewdly with [the Israelites], or they will increase and, in the event of war, join our enemies and fight against us and escape from the land." Therefore, the Egyptians set taskmasters over the Hebrews to oppress them with forced labor. The primary target in an oppressive society is the black male.

Look at verses 15 and 16, in Exodus 1. The king of Egypt said to the Hebrew midwives, "When you act as midwives to the

Hebrew women, and see them on the birthstool, [that is the same kind of birthing stool that they still use in Ghana] if it is a boy, kill him; but if it is a girl, she shall live." The males, the boys, the men are the primary target in an oppressive society that sees black men as a dangerous threat.

I am convinced that there is some stuff that you are just not able to see and some stuff you are not able to understand until after you are grown up. Paul said, "When I was a child, I spoke like a child, I thought like a child, I reasoned like a child" (1 Corinthians 13:11). When Moses was a child, he thought like a child. He thought he was different from those other Hebrews because of where he was privileged to live. He thought like a child. He thought he was better than those other Hebrews because he was blessed to live in a palace, while they lived in poverty. He thought like a child. He thought he lived in splendor, and that those Hebrews lived in squalor because they were lazy, they were ignorant, they were welfare queens and shiftless absentee fathers. To Moses, they had no sense of responsibility and nobility like the folk who were raising him.

He thought like a child. Moses looked right at oppression every day, but he did not realize what he was looking at because he wasn't oppressed. Moses reasoned like a child. He understood as a child, and he probably heard stupid conversations around the palace as the oppressors asked the question, "Why do they hate us?" "They hate us because we live so well off and they have to get up and go to work every day." There is some stuff that you are just not able to see or to understand, even while looking right at it, surrounded by it every day, until after you have grown up.

Moses was surrounded by oppression. Moses was born under oppression. Moses was miraculously kept from murder in an oppressive society. Moses grew up seeing the Hebrews oppressed, but Moses did not have a clue about what was happening until after he had grown up. In Exodus 2:11, it says, "One day, after

Moses had grown up." Moses went out to his people and saw their oppression. He saw, in other words, what he had been looking at but not really seeing. He saw their forced labor. He saw an Egyptian beating a Hebrew. We have a lot of folks in the United States of America who, like Moses, need to grow up and see what's really happening.

What the text says next is open to two different interpretations. Verse 12 says, "He looked this way and that, and seeing no one...." In other words, one interpretation is that he followed the Egyptian who had been beating the Hebrew until there was no one around or no one in sight (so he thought). The text says he saw no one. Or, interpretation number two is that there was no one around—except the Egyptian who was doing the beating and the Hebrew who was getting the beating. Now, look at the two different possible ways of interpreting this text.

If, according to the first interpretation, Moses followed the Egyptian until he thought they were alone, then that means that there is always somebody who sees what you are doing when you think nobody knows what you are doing. But, if the second interpretation is the real case (if there was nobody around except the one putting the hurt on somebody and the one being hurt by an unjust situation), then that means, as we see a bit later in the Scripture passage, that the very one you are trying to help will hurt you rather than hurt the system that is keeping him oppressed. The text says, "When he went out the next day, he saw two Hebrews fighting; and he said to the one who was in the wrong, 'Why do you strike your fellow Hebrew?' He answered, 'Who made you a ruler and judge over us? Do you mean to kill me as you killed the Egyptian?' Then Moses was afraid and thought, 'Surely the thing is known.' When Pharoah heard of it, he sought to kill Moses."

When it comes to an oppressive situation, or, more accurately, when it comes to people under oppression, look how they act.

When it comes to people under oppression, the very one you are trying to help—the oppressed—will turn on you and hurt you. All too often, they will turn on the one who helped them, rather than hurt the system that is keeping them oppressed. Or they will turn on the one who is helping them rather than the one who is hurting them. When it comes to an oppressive situation, what the text teaches us is that the oppressed end up fighting the wrong enemies.

I think a lot of this is related to what Dr. Asa Hillard, an imminent black psychologist, said in one of his books entitled *The Black Maroon*. In that book, there is a two-page chapter on the making of a sheepdog. (Dr. Hilliard learned this while watching the Discovery Channel.) At birth, they take a sheepdog (a German Shepherd, a Collie, or whatever) away from the litter it was born into and put it in a sheep litter so that it will suck on the breasts of a sheep. Here is the reasoning: Get the sheep's milk into the dog's system, get the sheep's DNA into its system, let it grow up along with that litter, let the dog play with that sheep litter, let it become just like that litter, and, when it gets grown, if a dog from its own litter comes near the sheep, it will attack the dog. If the master comes near threateningly, that dog will kill its own master to protect the sheep.

If you are missing the point, look at it this way. If you take (at birth) a Clarence Thomas or a J. C. Watts away from their own people, feed them at the breasts of Harvard and Yale, and let them get that DNA inside them, when their own people try to tell them what time it is, they will attack their own people, defending the very ones who are keeping them oppressed. You end up fighting the wrong enemies.

People under oppression turn *on* each other rather than turn *to* each other. That is, in essence, fighting the wrong enemy. You see black men turning on black men. That is fighting the wrong enemy. My brothers, you are the primary targets in an oppressive society that sees black men as a dangerous threat. Why are you fighting each other? You are fighting the wrong enemy. Biggie Smalls was fighting Tupac Shakur, and Tupac was fighting Biggie. They were fighting the wrong enemy. East Coast hip hop fighting West Coast gangsta rap. They are fighting the wrong enemies. Bloods fighting Crypts. They are fighting the wrong enemies.

Dr. Martin Luther King Jr., over thirty years ago, called America the number-one purveyor of violence in the world. Let me give you a hot clue in case you did not know. I ain't your enemy. I did not finance Noriega. I ain't your enemy. I did not finance Osama Bin Laden. I ain't your enemy. I did not allow the drugs to flow through Afghanistan. I ain't your enemy. I did not trade any arms for drugs in the Iran-Contra-Oliver North cover-up. I ain't your enemy. I did not put Nelson Mandela in prison, nor keep him there for twenty-seven years. I ain't your enemy. I did not ignore the hundreds of thousands of blacks killed in Rwanda, killed in Angola, killed in Mozambique. Brother man, I ain't your enemy.

I do not owe the United Nations one penny. I ain't your enemy. I did not conjure up the Tuskegee experience to kill hundreds of black men, injecting them with syphilis, and, in case you did not know, I did not invent the HIV/AIDS virus. I ain't your enemy. I do not control the CIA. I do not control the FBI. I do not control the National Security Council or any Special Forces. I am not your enemy. When you turn on me, you are fighting the wrong enemy, black man.

When black men turn on black men, they are fighting the wrong enemy. Look at what the text says. The one who was in the wrong is the one who "copped the attitude." Your brother is not oppressing you. Your brother did not enslave you. Your brother did not pass segregation laws, Jim Crow laws, apartheid laws, or a Supreme Court Dred Scott decision against you. Your brother did not define you as property—less than human or three-fifths of a man in the Constitution. Your brother did not make it a crime for you to learn how to read. Your brother did not say, "Kill the baby boys and let the girls live!"

In the text, Moses said to the one who was in the wrong, "Why do you strike your fellow Hebrew?" The one who was in the wrong copped an attitude. He then ran and told his master on one of his own to cover up his wrongdoing and to deflect attention away from himself. He said (in so many words), "Who died and left you in charge? What makes you think you're the ruler and judge over us? Your record ain't squeaky clean. You got some skeletons in your closet. I heard from a reliable source about what you have done."

When you confront folk with the Gospel in the present, and when they are in the wrong, they will quickly bring up some gossip from the past to confuse the issue. Confront them with the truth and they will try to confuse you with some trash. Rather than deal with the fact that Moses was right, brother man wanted to dredge up the past to prove that Moses was wrong yesterday. So he turns on another brother who is only trying to help him and finds himself, once again, fighting the wrong enemy.

The text teaches us three things: One, when you fight the wrong enemy, it puts you at odds with your allies. The very folk who are in your corner are the folk you will find yourself in conflict with. This puts you at odds with your allies.

First, to illustrate this point, there is this football analogy. You've got eleven men on the same team. The offense has the job of moving the ball ten yards this way in order to get a first down. Now, if they are on the twenty-five-yard line, if they can move it twenty-five yards, they are not only going to get a first down, but they are going to get a touchdown. In the huddle, the quarterback says, "I have noticed that every time I look to the left and every time I turn to the left, both linebackers and the defense commit to their right, my left, as if that is the way the play is going. So what I am going to call is a fake handoff to the left halfback, and then, after I fake it to him, I am going to turn and pitch it to my right halfback. I want the guard to pull with the fullback leading the blocking. Nobody is over there on the right but a defensive end, so we should easily get a first down and, depending on the blocking in the secondary, we might even get us a touchdown."

Eleven men, team effort, all allies. The ball is snapped. The quarterback turns to his left. The linebackers commit. The quarterback fakes a handoff to the left, spins and pitches it to the right of his tailback. The guard is pulling. The fullback is leading the blocking. Even the defensive end bought the fake to the left and he is too far out of place to stop and come back. They have a straight sweep right into the endzone. It is an automatic first down. Easy touchdown coming up when, suddenly, the fullback turns around and tackles his own teammate in the backfield and starts doing a victory shout in the backfield.

You are supposed to be on the same team. You are supposed to be working toward the same goals. You are allies and, instead of blocking for the man, here you are tackling the man on your own team. You are fighting the wrong enemy. You are at odds with your own ally. You are tackling your own teammate. When you are fighting the wrong enemy, it puts you at odds with your own allies. The very folk who are in your corner are the very folk you will find yourself in conflict with.

Okay. If football is not your game, then consider this illustration: Remember the analogy of the flock of geese? When a flock of geese flies, they fly as a team. They fly as a unit. They fly with one goal: to get from Point A to Point B. If you notice, the formation of a flock of geese is always in the shape of a "V," and there is one goose that is at the point of that "V." That is by design. The goose at the point of the "V," the lead goose, is creating a pocket of air current that makes flying for the rest of the flock much easier. The lead goose is hitting the headwinds straight on. The lead goose is being buffeted by the crosswinds, the down winds, and the wind shears. The lead goose is taking the punishment so that the other geese behind him or her can have an easier path through which to fly. They are all on the same team. They all have the same goal. They all fly with the same purpose: to get from Point A to Point B.

When the lead goose has been beat up too much, has been beaten down too much, or gets too tired to stay on the point and be buffeted any longer, it gives a signal and whoosh—a teammate, an ally, another goose, shifts position with it to take the point and give the leader some rest. But they do not stop flying. They are all on the same team. They all have the same goal. They are all flying with the same purpose: to get from Point A to Point B.

If a goose gets sick, if a goose gets tired, if a goose gets hurt, or if a goose gets wounded, they don't let that goose go down to the ground all by itself. Two other geese at a minimum, sometimes three, sometimes four, go down with the tired goose or the wounded goose, and they stay with the one who had to drop out until that one is strong enough to get back up and resume flying again. Or they will stay with the goose until it dies so that it will not have to die alone. Geese got more sense than people!

If the goose dies, the ones that went down with him wait until another flock flies overhead, and then they join that flock, so they continue flying as a team. They all have the same goal. They all have the same purpose: to get from Point A to Point B.

Whenever you hear all of that infernal noise coming from a flock of geese, moreover, it is not just background noise. It is not just needless noise. The geese in the back of the "V" formation are honking their encouragement to the goose that is up on the point. They are saying, "Honk! Go ahead. Honk! You are doing a good job. Honk, honk! We got your back. Honk, honk! Let us know when you need some help or you need some rest."

Don't you wish church folk had as much sense as geese? Don't you wish folk under oppression had as much sense as geese? They are all in the same predicament. All in slavery, all under oppression, and they are all on the same team. They are all supposed to have the same goal: to get from Point A (slavery) to Point B (freedom.) But geese don't fight the wrong enemy like people do. Geese don't get at odds with their own allies. Geese don't pull out of formation or pull off by themselves and run and tell the hunters which way the flock went. Geese don't get confused like people. When you fight the wrong enemy, it puts you at odds with your own allies. The very folk who are in your corner are the very folk you find yourself in conflict with when you are fighting the wrong enemy.

Then, second, this text teaches us that you end up hurting the one who is trying to help when you fight the wrong enemy. Moses was trying to help his people who were under oppression. Now, either the one who was getting beaten ran and told on him, or the one who was in the wrong ran and told. But whichever one ran and told on him, they ended up hurting the very one who was only trying to help them. Imagine how this country would be if brothers hadn't fought the wrong enemies during these insurrections. Do you know that there were over 300 rebellions, over 300 insurrections, over 300 revolts in North America by enslaved Africans who wanted to be free? The largest of those revolts were by Gabriel Prosser in 1800, Denmark Vesey in 1822, and Nathaniel Turner in 1829, 1830, and 1831. In all of those slave revolts, led by black Christian preachers, the revolts were stopped by an African running to tell "Massah what them darkies were getting ready to do." They were fighting the wrong enemy, and they ended up hurting the very ones who were only trying to help them.

Asa Hillard was right. The Discovery Channel was right. Our allegiance is to the oppressor and not to the oppressed. When you fight the wrong enemy, you end up hurting the one who is trying to help. Let me put it another way. You end fighting against the one you should be fighting beside.

I heard Rev. A. Lewis Patterson of Houston, Texas, put it this way fifteen years ago. Dr. Patterson said that being married or being in a relationship is like being in a boxing match. As a black man, you are still the primary target in an oppressive society that sees black men as a dangerous threat. So every day that you are out there in the ring, and while you are in the ring, you are in the crosshairs of the rifle of oppression. You are in the crosshairs of the rifle of racial profiling. You are in the crosshairs of the rifle of low expectations. You are in the crosshairs of the rifle of needing more education to get less pay than somebody you trained, who is now your boss, on the basis of their skin color. You are getting whipped every day from the time the bell rings in the morning until you can stumble back home into your corner at night. And when you stagger into your corner at night—beat up, tired, scarred, bloody, exhausted, tired of folk fighting you and beating up on you—you expect to sit down on your stool and have those who are there in your corner give you some water, refresh you, revive you, renew you, inspire you, and tell you that you can make it. Then, you can get on back up and go on back out into the ring the next day and face whatever it is that the next day has to bring. Black men in America, you need experienced brothers who have fought this fight of oppression in your corner. Don't turn from them; embrace them.

You do not expect, nor do you need, the folk who are supposed to be in your corner, the folk who are supposed to be helping you, taking that stool and knocking you upside your head between the rounds. You don't need them cutting you up some more, making you bloodier than you were when the bell rang at the end of the last round. That is fighting the wrong enemy. The folk who are supposed to be in your corner end up hurting you. Black men, we must face this demon of self-hatred if we are to stop fighting the wrong enemy!

Finally, the third thing this text teaches is that when you fight the wrong enemy, it keeps you from ever getting around to fighting the right fights. The people under oppression in this text, in Moses' day, had a difficult time getting around to fighting the right fights. They wanted to fight Moses and Aaron. A slave mentality will do that to you. It will mess you up so badly that you won't even know which fights are the right fights anymore. You will be fighting for the oppressor rather than fighting to end oppression. You will be taking votes to go back to Egypt. You will be fighting the folks who are attempting to set you free.

Do you have any idea what the right fights are today? We ought to be fighting for the minds of our young people. We've got teenagers who think their identities are tied up with which brand names they've got on their backs. We need to be fighting for the minds of our young people. We've got some teenagers whose self-esteem is wrapped up in FUBU and Air Jordan. I heard a young man tell his mother that he wasn't going to wear shoes from Payless. They had to be from Footlocker, and, if the shoes didn't cost over $150.00, he wasn't going to wear them because he would be embarrassed. We need to be fighting for the minds of our young people.

We need to be fighting for free health care for all of God's children. Regardless of their skin color and regardless of their ability to pay, all of God's children need and deserve quality health care. These are the right fights. We need to be fighting for free medicine for AIDS patients. If they can win that fight in South Africa, if they can win that fight in Brazil, then surely we can win that fight in North America, because God is the same God here as God is there. But we are too busy fighting the wrong fights. Black men, we must accept our purpose as men and fight for the future of our families and communities.

We need to be fighting for quality education for every citizen based on their ability to learn, not on their ability to pay. I have said this before, and I am going to keep on saying it until somebody hears me and comes and stands and fights beside me, joining me in this right fight. We need to be fighting against ignorance. We need to be fighting against intolerance. We need to be fighting against arrogance. We need to be fighting against discrimination. We need to be fighting against greed. We need to be fighting against racism. We need to be fighting against stereotypes. We need to be fighting against the desire for revenge. We need to be fighting against nationalism, and against hatred of folk who don't look like us, who don't talk like us, and who don't worship like us. These are just a few of the real fights. The right fights.

These are some of the things we need to be fighting for and fighting against. But we, my brothers, are so busy fighting the wrong enemies that we never seem to get around to fighting the right fights. Let me suggest to you that one of the primary ways of getting refocused, so that we can stop fighting the wrong fights, is to stop and turn aside as Moses does in the very next chapter, to put God back on our agenda.

God is not mentioned until the end of the second chapter of Exodus, when the people of promise discover that they ought to be asking God for help in this situation. It is not until chapter 3 that God gets Moses' attention from a burning bush in Midian. We, like they, have left the Living God out of the equation in the fights we are fighting. And to the extent that we continue to do that, we, my brothers, will keep on fighting the wrong enemies and fighting the wrong fights.

When you put God back in the equation, it takes you off of center stage and forces you to realize and recognize that each day you have is a gift from God, that each breath you take is a gift from God, and that you would not be where you are now if it were not for God. And then, instead of getting up every morning mad and thinking about how you want to get back at who you're going to get back at (or how you are going to get you some paybacks), with the focus on God, you can get up each day thanking God for another day.

You can get up each day, affirming that every day that God gives you is a day of thanksgiving. You can get up and put the focus back on God by saying, "This is the day the LORD made; I will rejoice and be glad in it." You can get up with confidence because the Word of God says that all you have to do is to ask God while believing. You can get up praying, "God, I have lost focus, fall fresh on me. I am fighting the wrong fights, fall fresh on me. Break me! I have gotten hard on the inside. Melt me! I have gotten rigid in my thinking. Mold me! You are the potter. Fill me! I need your Spirit. I cannot do it on my own. I need your Spirit to fall fresh on me."

chapter three

boys II men

walter s. thomas

∞

You were taught to put away your former way of life, your old self, corrupt and deluded by its lusts, and to be renewed in the spirit of your minds, and to clothe yourselves with the new self, created according to the likeness of God in true righteousness and holiness. (Ephesians 4:22–24, NRSV)

∞

it goes without saying that male children are considered a prize in most societies. In ancient society, women and girls were considered to be property and thus were owned by the men. Sick children and female babies were often carried outside the city and left there to die. Now, do not get me wrong; I am not saying that this is right or good, but it is a fact. Fathers often want a boy, and mothers are also guilty of the same desire. Male children are given a certain place, a special place, in the hierarchy of our respect.

Even in the training of children, this sense of a double standard is evident. Girls are taught to be chaste and pure, while boys are told to use protection and be cautious. We want male children to learn to be tough, competitive, smart, aggressive, and prepared. We do not want sons to be weak, effeminate, shy, or bashful. There is an image to which they must aspire and which serious parents try to reinforce.

And yet, as we look at the boys of our society, as we look at those youngsters on the doorstep of manhood, it is hard to conclude that they are the valuable assets that our culture has declared them to be. There are so many young men whose lives are tornadoes spinning wildly out of control. There are too many young men caught in the grip of ghetto gunfights and community crime. These assets, these pearls of tremendous price, have seemingly been devalued and depreciated.

So grave is this trend that a whole new type of "manhood" has grown up in our community; a whole new rite-of-passage program has been developed and implemented right under our noses. A new ethos has overtaken the minds and morals of our era, and now African American boys are becoming something—but the question is "What?" The Scriptures correctly conclude, "As a man thinketh, so is he…," and much of the desperate conditions that we are witnessing today are due to the fact that a new thinking pervades our generation.

There is a new standard for behavior, a new system of acceptability, a new approach to living that is alien to everything the older generations held as dear and true. Our youngsters, especially male children, are taught to be "def" and "yo"; they are taught to defend their turf and to fight for their homeboys. They are taught not to take anything from anybody, and to return every grievance with even greater force. Young black men often use guns to settle arguments, they smoke crack to avoid reality, and they use women to measure up to someone else's definition of respectability.

Let me add that it does not matter whether you live in the heart of the suburbs, or in the heart of the inner city, or on the doorstep of these kinds of sad realities; everyone is affected by this changing sense—this depreciating sense—of morality. The winds of behavior are now blowing from a new direction, an unfamiliar direction, an ungodly direction.

One of the terms that our young men use, a term that has deep meaning for them, is the phrase "You the man." Some young men have been known to kill so that this label could be hung on them by their peers. They must have "respect," but this respect is not the kind that we know and have grown up seeking to maintain. Too many of our young African American men speak of some form of power that they have renamed "respect," whereby others fear or revere them, and they act as if they are, as the phrase erroneously implies, "the man."

My fear is that such training and such living have us taking many—too many—trips to the cemetery, thus producing a generation of people for whom there will be no productive place in society and, in the words of our parents, who are "fattening frogs for snakes." We are seeing grown men act like teenagers, and persons who are advanced in years are still "bopping" and "pimping" as if they are still a part of a generation that has long since passed.

If the world is to be recaptured from the snare of the devil that has taken it captive, real men will be required, and this means that we have to start turning boys to men. There is only one way to go in turning boys to men. There is only one guide to follow. We do not turn boys to men simply with degrees from our various colleges and universities. It is not just a matter of securing a job with one of the Fortune 500 companies. It is not "being the man" in the "'hood." There is only one way to turn boys to men. The apostle Paul spells it out for us in his letter to the church at Ephesus: "Put away your former way of life, your old self, corrupt and deluded by its lusts, ... be renewed in the spirit of your minds, ... clothe yourself with the new self, created according to the likeness of God..." (Ephesians 4:22–24).

The church of Paul's day was embroiled in a battle. Ephesus was the Vanity Fair of the world. Ephesus was known for its strange practices and its loose ways. Yet it was here that God sent Paul to proclaim the Gospel. Now, some time later, Paul writes to them and encourages them to remember that Ephesus must be turned around, and if it is to happen, they, too, must be turned around. When Paul was there, God used him to preach with such power that souls were saved and many were brought to faith. Yet what was convicting to Paul's hearers was not just his message, but also his manhood.

Some of us do not realize that, although we have to communicate the Gospel, it must come through a mature personality. Paul not only had a word, but his life reflected the true measure of a godly man. There is no doubt that spirituality can make you mature, but we ought not see it as a substitute for maturity. It is not a case of spirituality versus maturity; it is that spirituality operates within and through a mature person. The true age of a man cannot be found on his birth certificate, but it will be reflected in his maturity in the context of his understanding of God. I have seen many men who were in the church but who were still immature. They were baby boys who needed to be diapered, spoon-fed, placated, and made the center of attention. Just because some men come to church, attend study, and are in discipleship, do not conclude that the brothers have moved from boys to men in the truest sense. There is more to being a man than this. In other words, "Hallelujahs" are no substitute for hard work. "Praise the Lord" is no substitute for providing for the family. "Thank you, Jesus" doesn't replace faithfulness and truth. Singing in the choir is no substitute for respect for others and treating people right. Being involved in the church does not guarantee successful involvement and relationships with people. In fact, real manhood is a mixture, a marriage, a union of maturity and a message.

You see, manhood is not a function of age, possessions, or degrees. It is a quality of life, along with a sense of forthrightness. It is the ability to know right from wrong and to do that which is right instead of constantly giving in to what is wrong. It is accepting responsibility and putting limits on freedom. It is dealing with anger and rage in a way that produces positive possibilities and potential. It is walking with kings and not losing the common touch. It is helping others and being there when they need you. It is not getting high, but handling and managing the lows. It is not running around, but knowing how to stand still. It is not just being jive, but having joy and knowing when to be serious. It is not falling for everything, but standing tall for something. And it is being honest, faithful, and truthful. That's what being a man is all about!

It is in this fourth chapter that Paul lays out his basic set of instructions for those who are new in the faith, whose aim it is to become mature Christians, steadfast and unmovable. Paul was well aware that it was time for the people of Ephesus to make a real change, and he was well aware that there would be a real tension between their new life and the world in which they lived. In order for the Ephesians to be the witnesses that God was calling for, they would have to have respect for God's work in their lives.

Let me add that, in order for the transformation to take place, God must be involved. The Psalmist declared, "How can young people keep their way pure? By guarding it according to your word. With my whole heart I seek you; do not let me stray from your commandments. I treasure your word in my heart, so that I may not sin against you" (Psalm 119:9–11, NRSV). There is no other way for a person to grow up and to grow up whole. Without God, there will always be a deficiency that is unresolved and unattended. The only way we will turn our city around is with a return to the admonitions of the Lord.

We have stressed getting everything but God in our lives. We have pursued the material things rather than the spiritual things. We have the cars, the houses, the clothes, the money, the jewelry, but what we don't have is a sense of God and his movements in our lives. We have everything except what it takes to make a man. We need the Lord to make men out of boys. Our society makes criminals; it makes self-centered egotists; it makes abusers; it makes addicts; it makes liars; and it makes users. But God can take a nobody and make him a somebody. God can take a loser and make him a winner. God can take a failure and make him a success. God can take a man who feels defeated and give him glorious victories. God can take an empty and lost man and fill that brother until he is overflowing. God can take a criminal and make that criminal a convert. God can take a drug addict and make him a respected member of the community. God can take a boy from the 'hood and make him the man of the year. God can take a school dropout and make him a G.E.D. graduate. God can take a man without a job and give him a sense of dignity and respect. God can take a struggling single father and make him proud of his efforts and accomplishments, no matter how great or how small.

It is no secret what the Lord can do. His record of success speaks for itself. My brothers in Christ, we must spend time making sure that our boys know the Lord. It is no longer permissible to allow the streets to be their principal instructor, where drug lords and street-smart crazies set the standard for our boys. If our boys are to reach manhood—true manhood—to take their place in society and become what they can be, then there must be a serious "God factor" in their lives. Brothers, we have to grow them and show them, using God as the example. Brothers must teach other brothers that the Bible says, "Your word is a lamp to my feet and a light to my path" (Psalm 119:105).

Let me add that men have to move beyond the notion that women are more spiritual and sensitive than men. Nothing is further from the truth. God is no respecter of persons. He ministers his spirit to each and every one. In fact, I challenge the prevailing thought that the church is just filled with women. This place has men, real men, real Christian men, real Christian God-fearing men who are not ashamed to speak of their love for him. It was the Lord who gave us a reason for living. It was the Lord who took the needle and gave us his name. It was the Lord who took the pain and gave us peace. It was the Lord who took us from the streets and gave us homes and families. And it was the Lord who took persons who were their own worst enemy and became their best friend. Only the Lord can make a man! For it was God who reached down into dust and created man, and breathed the gift of life into him, and made him into his image and likeness.

Paul does not stop his admonishment to the Christians at Ephesus. He says to them, words that the men of today also hear, "Put away your former way of life, your old self..." (Ephesians 4:22). In other words, we must retire our old ways. The apostle Paul makes an important claim in his letter to the church at Corinth. He said, "When I was a child, I spoke like a child, I thought like a child, I reasoned like a child; when I became an adult, I put an end to childish ways" (1 Corinthians 13:11). My brothers, when the Lord is growing you into manhood, as hard as it may appear, you have to let go of some of the old ways that brought you to the point where you needed the Lord. You see, our old ways are stumbling blocks to our growth. Our problem is that we don't know what we need to let go of or if we really want to let it go. You see, when many of us come to Christ, we refuse to give up everything. In fact, we try to be our same old selves, just with a little Christ in our lives. Yet, I tell you, as Christ becomes increasingly important in your life, the more you will realize that you have things to give up, the more you will find yourself making the hard and difficult decision to let them go. The difference now is that with Christ in your life, you understand why you are letting it go. It will still be hard, it will still be difficult, but you will know, because of who he is, that this is the best thing in the world for you.

We need to be honest with ourselves—some of our ways need to change. Manhood is knowing that the time has come to let some things go and to move on in seriousness and sincerity. We can't play basketball forever; there comes a time when we must let it go. We can't be jive forever; there comes a time when we must grow up and face responsibility. There are some things that we need to let go. And no time is better than today. We can't run from accountability forever; we eventually must take a stand for our beliefs.

Let me go one step further. When the Lord is real in your life, you are constantly retiring something. Now, some new area of our lives comes under scrutiny and we have to evaluate it in light of our whole life. One of the reasons that so many of our young men are being blown away and why so many are into corrupt practices is that they have not had an evaluation of their lives in light of the value of their lives. Too many brothers view themselves as expendable, as long as it earns them some attention. Well, God will give you all the attention you need. When you look at what you are doing and realize that there is someone who loves you and cares for you, then some—many—of those habits will change. Your desire for attention is all about self-gratification. But when you become a mature Christian man, your mindset evolves and moves from attention to intention. Our intentions dictate the righteousness of God manifesting himself in our lives.

I cannot say it enough: a new consciousness will produce new actions, and new actions turn boys to men. Finally, the apostle says, put on the new self, created to be like God. Don't just retire your old habits; redress your spirit in new ways! When God leads us to manhood, he does not just take from us the old ways; he replaces them with new ways, such as coming to worship, serving in the church, helping other people, praying and believing, reading the Word, attending Bible study, fellowshipping with the saints, telling truth instead of lies, shouting instead of stealing, crying instead of cursing, and succeeding instead of failing. New practices and new ways are what solidify the manhood that God is creating. In essence, the new ways purify; they help to rid us of the last vestiges of our old self. They keep us traveling on the right road. They have a way of keeping us from going backwards, from going from men to boys. They have a way of not allowing us to be content with any form of stagnation.

New practices make us productive. Our lives take on accomplishment when we redress our spirits. We see that we can do as the Lord said we could. We see results. We need new ways to accept our new self. We aren't really new until our behavior matches our beliefs.

Finally, new practices produce power. We can change this world because "greater is he that is within us than he that is in the world" (1 John 4:4). You cannot send a boy to do a man's job! It will take men to turn this world into the world that God wants it to be, and his spirit is all the power that we need. The best illustration of a man taking on "new ways" and displaying purity, productivity, and power is the shepherd boy David, who killed Goliath and eventually became King David. David, as a shepherd boy, heard Goliath talk about the God of Israel, and because of his loyalty to the God of Israel, David accepted the challenge to fight Goliath and produced a victory for the Lord and the people of Israel. After this victory, David knew it was the power of the spirit of God that helped him to defeat Goliath. David never again had to wonder about his own power because he knew that "If God is for us, who is against us?" (Romans 8:31). He knew that no weapon formed against him would prosper. Boys rely on their own strength; men rely on the strength of God.

chapter four

overlooked by many, SEEN by one

claude alexander

> Jesse made seven of his sons pass before Samuel, and Samuel said to Jesse, "The LORD has not chosen any of these." Samuel said to Jesse, "Are all your sons here?" And he said, "There remains yet the youngest, but he is keeping the sheep." And Samuel said to Jesse, "Send and bring him; for we will not sit down until he comes here." He sent and brought him in. Now he was ruddy, and had beautiful eyes, and was handsome. The LORD said, "Rise and anoint him; for this is the one." (1 Samuel 16:10–12, NRSV)

∞

if you were to ask people, "with the exception of Jesus, who is your favorite biblical character?" the name David would probably be mentioned the most. One reason would be that, with the exception of Jesus, no single character seems to take up more space in the Bible, just in terms of his story being told, than David. The story of David extends from 1 Samuel 16 to 1 Kings 2:10. It is further told in 1 Chronicles 11–29. David would also top the list because no other character looks more like us in so many ways than does David. In David we are able to see so much of ourselves and what it means to be who we are in relationship with God. We see ourselves in the images of David given in the Bible.

If I were to ask what images you recall concerning David, some would answer with the image of a shepherd boy, who, armed with only a slingshot, five smooth stones, and the name of the

Lord of hosts, defeated the giant named Goliath. Others would call to mind the image of David playing music in the court of Saul. A third group would mention the image of David and Saul riding through the village and the townspeople shouting, "Saul has killed his thousands, and David his ten thousands" (1 Samuel 18:7). There would be those who would place David's friendship with Jonathan before us as a memorable image. Still others would lay the image of David as a fugitive on the run from Saul. They might recall the times when David could have killed Saul, but refused to do so. We would all remember David bringing the ark into Jerusalem and dancing before the Lord. David's kindness to Mephibosheth would have to be mentioned. We could not forget the infamous balcony scene, which was the backdrop for his fateful fall with Bathsheba. Of course, there would also be the scene of Nathan's confronting David and David's repentance. As we bring those recollections to a close, someone else just might hasten to add David's flight from Absalom and his return.

All of these would be accurate remembrances of David. However, it wasn't until recently that I was moved by another image of David. It was one that I really hadn't considered before, because it seemed to be so far removed from the person we know as the man after God's own heart. While this image is one that is seldom considered, I believe that it is one which we need to notice in order to appreciate the other images of David, as well as to gain some perspective concerning our own lives. Before David stepped into any of the events for which we so fondly and readily remember him, he was in a different situation. Permit me to set the scene, my brethren.

We are caught in the midst of an unfolding drama. The people requested a king to lead them. In response to their request, the Lord gave them Saul, the son of Kish, to be their king. Initially, Saul served both the Lord and the people well. However, there came a time when Saul began to be casual with the sacredness of

his assignment and with his reverence toward God. He began to
be more concerned about himself and his position with the people than he was about his obedience to God. In that condition, he
began to disobey God, and for his disobedience, God rejected
him as king of Israel. That is where 1 Samuel 15 ends. Chapter
16 begins with the prophet Samuel crying over God's rejection of
Saul. He's stuck in a moment that God has already moved
beyond. It's a sad thing to be stuck in a moment that God has
already passed.

God assures Samuel that there is a replacement for Saul. He
directs Samuel to go to the town of Bethlehem and to find a man
by the name of Jesse. When he finds Jesse, Samuel is to give him
a particular message: "I have chosen one of his sons to be king."
In obedience to the word of the Lord, Samuel journeys to Bethlehem. When he arrives, he informs the elders that he has come
in peace to offer a sacrifice to the Lord and that he needs for Jesse
and his sons to be present. Having received the word concerning
the arrival of Samuel, Jesse makes his way with his seven sons.
When Jesse arrives, Samuel consecrates Jesse and his seven boys.
The seven stand before him with curiosity written upon their
faces. Upon the face of Jesse, there is a look of anticipation and
hope; the prophet Samuel has an interest in one of his sons! The
last time Samuel was looking for a man, it was to anoint him to
become king. Perhaps this is the purpose for this visit. Jesse begins
to imagine one of his seven sons as the next king of Israel.

The first son to catch the eyes of Samuel is Eliab, a rather dom-
inating individual. He seems to be chiseled brass. In Samuel's
mind, the thought is "Surely the LORD's anointed is now before
the LORD" (1 Samuel 16:6). Eliab just looks kingly. He has a regal
bearing and countenance about himself. As Samuel considers
Eliab and is about to make his announcement, the Lord inter-
rupts and says, "Do not look on his appearance or on the height
of his stature, because I have rejected him" (1 Samuel 16:7). The

Lord does not look at the things that man looks at. Rather, man looks at the outward appearance, but the Lord looks at the heart.

As Samuel is involved in a spiritual search, God warns him against being governed by fleshly considerations. Samuel is involved in God's selection of God's representative and leader. This is a divine work in progress. When you are looking for a participant in a spiritual work, fleshly considerations do not apply. Flesh can only give birth to flesh. Flesh can only reproduce the flesh. Flesh can only inspire the flesh. When it comes to the work of God, the flesh has no place. Eliab's appearance and height would be of no use to God if that at which God is looking—the heart—is wrong. While Eliab may have everything else, his heart is not right.

I want you to know that, in the things of God, you can have everything else going for you. You can have talent. You can have personality. You can be attractive to the masses of people. But if your heart is not right, if your heart is not in the right posture before God, everyone else may say "yes" to you, but God will say "no." While Samuel had said "yes" to Eliab, God said "no."

The next son, Abinadab, passes before Samuel. Again, the Lord says no. Shammah advances. Again, the Lord says negative. All seven sons come before Samuel, but none of them receives the Lord's approval. What a moment! Surely, one of them would have received a positive nod. Samuel begins to wonder whether or not he has heard the Lord correctly. God did tell him to go to Bethlehem and to see a man by the name of Jesse. God did tell him that one of Jesse's sons would be anointed to be king over Israel. Jesse, having been told of the event, brought seven sons to the prophet, yet none received the Lord's okay. What is going on here?

Finally, Samuel is led to ask Jesse, "Are all your sons here? Are there any other sons that you have?" Jesse responds, "There is still the youngest, but he is tending the sheep." There was another son that Jesse had seen fit to leave behind! He was not thought to be worth making the trip. This is born out in Jesse's terminology for this son: The term for youngest is *haqqaton*. It not only means youngest in terms of age, but it also means smallest in terms of size and lowest in terms of significance. David was the runt in the family. He was the one considered to be of least account. He was given the least important job on the farm, namely tending to the sheep. As David tended to sheep, he was out of the way. He was out of sight. Being out of sight kept him out of mind. Most of the time, David was ignored, passed by, and overlooked. With the prophet Samuel in town to anoint somebody, David was overlooked. He was ignored. He was a nonentity to his daddy and his brothers.

That's been the experience of many African American men. You've been overlooked. Perhaps it's been within your family. You weren't born first and you're not the baby. The oldest and the youngest get the attention. You feel overlooked. Perhaps it's due to the fact that brother or sister are straight-A students, star athletes, great singers, dynamic speakers, popular in school and in church, good looking or fine, and you're an average student. No one raves over you. No fuss is made about you. You're never the first one picked for anything. As a matter of fact, you're the last one picked. When it comes to parties or get-togethers, your name is hardly ever mentioned. It's an afterthought. Perhaps it's the case on your job. You try your best to be faithful to the company. You do all that you can to move the company forward. However, when it comes time for bonuses, when the time comes for promotions, you are overlooked. Your name is not mentioned. Your suggestions are not heeded. You feel overlooked.

Some brother, now, is still living with the stigma of being overlooked as a child. Within your mind is the image of that boy who was never asked out, that boy who was never picked. Tapes of your being unacceptable and unworthy continue to play over and over in your mind. You can't have a healthy relationship. You can't market yourself as someone of value because of the pain of being overlooked. It is of great assurance to know that before David became the slayer of giants, the psalmist of Israel, the great king of Israel, he was considered to be a runt. He was overlooked by many, but seen by One.

Overlooked by his daddy, overlooked by his brothers, unknown to Samuel, but seen by God! There is David, running along the Judean hillside tending to the sheep. In his obscurity, God takes notice of him. While everyone looks at Eliab, Abinadab, and Shammah, God's eyes are on David. No one else's eyes may be on you, my brothers, but you need to know that God's eyes are on you. That's the first lesson: No one else may notice you, but God is taking notice.

David was seen by God. God was observing on a level that others missed. They missed the level of David's heart. No, he did not have Eliab's stature. No, he did not have Abinadab's speed. No, he did not have Shammah's *savoir faire.* However, none of them had David's heart. That's what God saw that Jesse and everyone else missed. For God, the heart is what is primary. Let me suggest to you that in this decision God gives us a clear example of what is primary when searching for anything that is lasting. You had better look at the heart. Regardless of how fine, how cute, how smart, how talented, you had better look at the heart. In the remoteness of the Judean hills, God was able to see David's heart. David would write in Psalm 139, "O LORD, you have searched me and known me. You know when I sit down and when I rise up; you discern my thoughts from far away. You search out my path and my lying down, and are acquainted with all my ways. Even before a word is on my tongue, O LORD, you know it completely" (Psalm 139:1–4). Left behind and overlooked by men, David was seen by God. God looked at the condition of David's heart.

As he looked at David's heart, God saw several things. While David had what would be considered to be the menial job, it was the means by which God was able to develop a good heart in David and through which God would then examine David's heart. My African American brothers, I don't care how menial you may think your lot to be, know that it is the grounds whereupon God is able to develop you and from which God will examine your fitness for elevation. God never elevates without examining you first.

God examined the heart of David and the first thing that God saw was patience. Herding sheep takes time. Sheep can be unnerving sometimes. They do stupid things. They get caught in holes and vines and wires for no other reason than stupidity. A shepherd must rescue them from their stupidity. Furthermore, the rewards of being a shepherd are not immediate. Before the sheep are sheared and sold for meat, they must be fed, searched for, and protected from thieves and wolves. A shepherd must know how to wait. David learned the art of waiting. That's why he could say, "Wait for the Lord; be strong, and let your heart take courage; wait for the LORD!" (Psalm 27:14).

God also saw responsibility in David. David was responsible with the task that his father gave him. No, it wasn't the most important task. No, it wasn't the most glamorous task. No, it did not gather a great deal of attention. Yet David treated his job as if it were the most important job around. He was as responsible with it as he would be if he were the king of Israel. God saw in David a level of responsibility with which he could trust his people. Because David could be trusted with his daddy's sheep, David could be trusted with God's people.

It is when you are in an overlooked position that God can see how trustworthy you really are. He is able to see the real reason you do what you do. Do you carry out your responsibilities because you are responsible, or just because someone is watching you and you want admiration or praise? Do you worship and serve because you love the Lord, or because you want people to think that you are so spiritual? It is important to honor God in the small tasks. Go to work. Pay the bills. Go to class. Be faithful to your spouse. Be faithful in the small things. My brothers, it is only when you are faithful in little things that God is willing to trust you with bigger things. In Luke 16:10, Jesus declares, "Whoever is faithful in a very little is faithful also in much; and whoever is dishonest in a very little is dishonest also in much."

The third thing that God saw in David was humility. David was not born the first son of a king. He was the eighth son of a farmer. As his brothers stood in front of the prophet Samuel, he was in the middle of nowhere tending sheep. This developed within him humility of heart. David could be obedient. He could be led and taught by God. Saul was rejected by God because of his lack of humility. He became lifted in pride and began to disobey God. God saw humility within David, which would be necessary in leading the people of God.

While Jesse overlooked David, God saw David's heart and moved Samuel to instruct Jesse to call David forward. Jesse and David's brothers told David to stay behind, but God called David forward. That's another point: When your heart is right before God, while you may be overlooked, God will call you forward in his time for his purpose.

The command goes out to get David from the sheep. The prophet Samuel wants to see him. God is calling David from obscurity, from the shadows of his misapplied purpose. He is calling him from the background to the foreground. He is getting ready to move David forward. He is getting ready to move him upward. He is preparing to move David onward. When God sees a heart of integrity, a heart of faithfulness, a heart of patience, a heart of humility, a heart of responsibility, God issues the call to come forward, to move upward and onward.

Samuel sends for David. He says that they will not sit down until David arrives. They wait for his arrival. For some man right now who's been overlooked, whom God has been preparing, I want you to know that God has a group waiting on your arrival. There's an employer waiting on your arrival. There's a wife waiting on your arrival. There are children waiting on your arrival. There's a house waiting on your arrival. There are brothers and sisters waiting on your arrival. There are mothers and fathers waiting on your arrival. There are ministries waiting on your arrival. God's been preparing you in the midst of obscurity, in the midst of having been overlooked. Now he is getting ready to bring you forth. God and his people await your arrival. What God has planned cannot go forward until God brings you there. It does not matter how long that it seems that it is taking for you to arrive, what God has planned for you to receive yet awaits your arrival. No one can move it. No thief can steal it. No demonic force can destroy it. God holds it for you. God maintains it for you. Black men in America, realize that God has not forgotten about you. God has a plan, a purpose, and a promise just for you.

Look at the scene. Samuel, Jesse, and the boys all await David's arrival. The folks who left David behind are now made to wait for David to show up. It's interesting that Jesse took his seven eldest sons. He took what he thought would be the complete presentation to Samuel. God rejected all seven of them and called for the eighth son. God was doing a new thing. In doing a new thing, God required that which signified a new beginning, being the eighth son of Jesse. David was overlooked by many but seen by one, in part, because Jesse was operating according to the status quo. Jesse was operating in the "business as usual" mode. But God was doing a new thing. God was starting something fresh and novel. Some black man has been overlooked because he doesn't fit the status quo. The good news for you, my fellow men, is that God has you set up for a new thing. God wants to start something with you. God wants to initiate something with you.

God wants to launch something with you. God wants to make a shift and use you as his instrument.

Suddenly, the men begin to see the small frame of a young man approaching them. His features become more and more distinct. As Samuel looks, he sees a young lad with ruddy hair, fine features, and handsome. The Lord says, "Rise and anoint him; for this is the one." Samuel takes the horn of oil and anoints David in the presence of his brothers. He is anointed in the presence of those who called him a runt, in the presence of those who overlooked him, in the presence of those who cast him aside, in the presence of those who left him by the wayside. From that day on, the spirit of the Lord came upon David in power. That's the next point: God will give you what you need when he calls you forward.

God will supply an anointing for the assignment. Imagine, a young shepherd boy given the task of being the king of Israel! He would certainly need an anointing for that assignment. God anoints him, and the Spirit rests upon him in power. All of David's God-directed appointments were accompanied by a fresh anointing from God. It is after David was anointed that we are given his name. This signifies that, before the anointing of the Lord, his name did not matter. It would not be *through* God that David would rule; it would be *under* the anointing of the Lord. With the anointing of the Lord, David could be what God would have him to be.

Some African American man today is worried about whether he is up to what the Lord has in store for him. You wonder if you have what it takes. Brothers, I want you to know that you are not the important factor. It is the anointing that God has for the assignment that is important. Under the anointing of God, you are more than a conqueror. Under the anointing of God, you are a victor. Under the anointing of God, you are a giant killer. Under the anointing of God, you are a demon slayer. God has an anointing for the assignment. Whatever he has assigned unto your hands, there is a corresponding anointing. There's an anointing to grow the business. There's an anointing to develop the ministry. There's an anointing to raise the children. There's an anointing to lead the family. There's an anointing to reclaim the neighborhood.

Finally, not only are we made to know that while you might be overlooked by men, you are not overlooked by God and that when God sees integrity of heart within you, God will bring you forward in his time to accomplish his purpose. Brothers, know that God will give you what you need for that purpose, but we are also made to know something else: When God anoints you, people will recognize his presence in your life.

After David is anointed, Samuel goes to Ramah. The scene shifts to Saul. Under the judgment of God, Saul is tormented by an evil spirit. He needs somebody to soothe him by playing music. One of his servants tells him that there is a son of Jesse who knows how to play a harp. He is a brave man and a warrior. He speaks well and is fine-looking. And the Lord is with him. The young man about whom the servant speaks is David. Before the event with Samuel, no one noticed him. No one thought about him. No one considered him. Now, the anointing of the Lord is upon him. The presence of the Lord is seen within him. It cannot be overlooked. Before the anointing, he was known as the runt. He was considered to be inconsequential. Now, he is a brave man and a warrior.

The one person who cannot be overlooked is the Lord. When he dwells within you, when his anointing is upon your life, it cannot be overlooked. It will be recognized. It will be acknowledged. When it is seen, the presence of the Lord will make an avenue for you. The Lord's presence will open up things for you. When people see the God in you, things begin to happen. It was the God in Joseph that got Potiphar's attention. It was the God in Joseph that got the cupbearer's attention. It was the God in Joseph that got Pharaoh's attention. It was the God in Daniel that got Nebuchadnezzar's attention. It was the God in Daniel that got Belshazzar's and Darius' attention. Many people and institutions might overlook you, but the God in you cannot be overlooked. Brothers, God cannot be ignored! "The heavens are telling the glory of God; and the firmament proclaims his handiwork. Day to day pours forth speech, and night to night declares knowledge" (Psalm 19:1–2). Some man today can surely testify that, when people have overlooked you, the presence of the Lord took over. The presence of the Lord made the way. The presence of the Lord made the connection.

Perhaps knowing that David was overlooked is not enough. Well, there is another who is in the line of David. He, too, was overlooked. He came to his own, and his own received him not. He was overlooked in his own hometown. He was overlooked by the Pharisees and the priests. Nevertheless, the Lord knew him: he was his only begotten son. The spirit of the Lord was upon him. Even though Jesus was overlooked by many, God brought him forth to be the captain of our salvation, the author and the finisher of our faith. The God in him gave him the victory at Calvary. He now has a name that's above every name. Now, his name is the only name given whereby we must be saved. Soon, every knee will bow and every tongue will confess that he is Lord to the glory of God the Father. Soon, every eye will behold him.

Thank God for that name. One day, I called on his name. He looked upon me and gave me salvation. He looked upon me and gave me his spirit. I thank God for his presence in my life! His presence has made the difference. His presence can't be ignored. His presence can't be overlooked. His presence is my joy. His presence is my strength. His presence is my peace. His presence makes the difference!

chapter five

a father's KISS:
men need to be loved, too

james c. perkins

So he set off and went to his father. But while he was still far off, his father saw him and was filled with compassion; he ran and put his arms around him and kissed him. (Luke 15:20, NRSV)

∞

the greatest tragedy that affects us as african American people is that our family life—family as we have traditionally understood it—has almost fizzled out. If we were to scroll the "misery index" as we would on a computer screen, we would see one dire statistic after another regarding our family structure. One of the most alarming of those statistics is the fact that close to eighty percent of our families are headed by single females. Beyond divorce, these women are single for one of several reasons: They were never married to the man who fathered their children; the father became addicted to drugs or became trapped in the grip of alcohol and abandoned the home; the father decided to pursue an "alternative" or homosexual lifestyle; the father is incarcerated; or the father is dead.

Now, if eighty percent of our families are headed by women, that puts the men who are married with children in a very select group. They are part of the twenty percent who are trying to admirably live out the experience of family life. But, there is a word of caution that needs to be delivered to that select twenty percent: Even though they are physically present, they are often emotionally absent.

The cause of this emotional absenteeism is, in large part, due to the fact that most men, especially black men, have not been trained and nurtured to know how to handle their feelings in the context of relationships. Men know how to be angry. They know how to laugh, even when there is nothing funny. Men have learned to laugh to keep from crying. But too many of our women say that their men do not know how to open up and express their true feelings; too many men do not know how to pursue intimacy in their relationships.

Sadly, a lot of men still have not grown up emotionally. They are still boys, in the play stage. These are the men who get off of work on Friday and, instead of enjoying that early weekend time with their families, they prefer to go to the club or to the bar and spend time with "the boys." They know how to play at their family relationships, but they do not know how to work at relationships.

Too many men were not raised to know how to handle their emotions and how to connect with their feelings. They did not learn that. And it is not the job of the mother to teach them. Mothers, most definitely, contribute to the emotional development of their sons. Most men can think back over the years and recall how their mothers, during moments of turmoil, would gather them to their breasts and wipe away their tears, while assuring them that things would work out. Mothers play an important role in the lives of their children; mothers provide their children with emotional security. They comfort and reassure their sons when those boys are assaulted by strong emotions.

Fathers, by contrast, should be teaching their sons to *handle* their feelings. They contribute to the emotional development of their sons in a different way. They stir and agitate the feelings and emotions of their boys. And, all too often, the feelings and emotions that the father nurtures are aggressive and tend toward violence. The father, in play—which is the first way that fathers begin interacting and relating to their sons—teaches his son how to box or to be rough and tough. It starts out playfully, at first, but then it escalates. It gets almost to a panic point where the son does not know how far this "play" is going to go. The father is developing certain emotions in his son so that the child will know how far to go. So, when the son is older and is out on the playground and another child confronts him, those feelings that the father has put in him while playing and roughhousing come to the surface. The son knows how to handle those aggressive situations. However, our sons need to be taught that being sensitive to women, children, and each other involves more manhood than anything else.

The problem is that fathers minimize the more tender and loving emotions. They are afraid that nurturing those types of emotions will make their sons effeminate and less of a man. Instead, sons are taught that, when it comes to relationships, they should keep those more tender feelings to themselves or to ignore such feelings. When a close family member dies, they are not to shed a tear; they are to handle it "like a man." In fact, men are discouraged from showing hurt or pain when they are physically hurt. When a son falls from his bicycle and there is a gash in his knee, he is told to hold in any expression of pain and to act as if he does not feel the hurt. He is taught not to cry or display any emotion. He is raised to be an "ice man," to don a façade of being cool.

For men, this "bottling up" translates into pain and hurt in marital relationships and families because they were not taught how to handle their loving emotions. They cannot express their feelings within the context of emotional intimacy. Men frequently do not feel comfortable being close to someone. Those gentle feelings were never truly developed so that when those feelings start to well up inside them, they do not know what to do with them and, often, do not even know what they are. This creates a state of perpetual stress and anxiety that all too often manifests itself in a lack of expression toward the people and things that a man loves the most.

This has to change! Some healing has to take place in our lives, black men. Right now, today, men are being challenged to venture into new emotional territory. They must cover new ground. They can find the tools for this healing from the Gospel of Luke, in this climactic passage from the parable of the prodigal son: "So he set off and went to his father. But while he was still far off, his father saw him and was filled with compassion; he ran and put his arms around him and kissed him" (Luke 15:20).

This passage, which shows the father greeting the returning boy, who had left home after breaking all ties with his father, demonstrates a valuable and important lesson for all men. It is all right for fathers to show love for their sons; it is all right for men to open up and share their emotions with their wives and families.

In this parable, before the emotional reunion, the son had ruined any relationship he may have had with his father. He had taken one third of what his father had accumulated, had run off, and then squandered it all. The son had been a prince and then found himself wallowing in the lowest estate. He was working in a pigpen! He ended up living as a pig and trying to succeed as a pig. In today's world, that is equivalent to trying to succeed as a junkie or an alcoholic, and dropping out from life. It cannot happen. There is no successful junkie; there is no successful alcoholic. The prodigal had failed as a son, and he had failed as a person. Then, to quote the parable, the son "came to himself." And he said, "You know, I've messed up badly, but I'm going back to the one person who has always taken care of me and who has always shown me love. I'm going back to my father."

This is where we pick up this parable. The father was now an old man. But when he saw his son, he pulled up his robe, gathered up his strength, and ran to meet his boy. The son could not even get to the house first because the father ran out to meet him. The father caught the son, hugged him, and kissed him on the neck. Another translation says that the father just kept on kissing him, and kissing him, and kissing him. He kissed his son fervently. Black men need to give back the emotionless attitudes that we have inherited from other cultural groups. We need to reclaim our sense of oneness. The Bible says that Jesus prayed that they might be one with one another as the Father and Son are one.

The kiss, in this parable, is a symbol of the expression of intense emotion and joy. Now, of course, we do not actually expect men to begin greeting each other with a kiss on the neck. Kissing on the neck is not an accepted greeting in our culture, such as when a male lightly kisses someone on both cheeks as is common in some European and Mediterranean cultures. But the symbolism in this parable carries a crucial lesson for African American males. When the father "put his arms around him and kissed him," that was a symbolic embrace that said, "Son, I love you." Men need that experience! They need the significant males in their lives to, in effect, "kiss them on the neck"—to hug them and say to them, "Son, brother, nephew—whomever—I love you." They need to feel what it is like to feel loved and wanted. They need to feel those kinds of emotions so that they will know how to appropriately express them in intimate situations. It is hard for a man to allow himself to be in an attachment with anyone if he has never been given a sense of attachment from the important men in his life.

Before a man can be a beloved husband, he must first be a beloved son. We need to practice sharing intimate thoughts and feelings between fathers and their sons. We can find this love in the Scriptures. In Matthew 3:17, after Jesus is baptized, God the father expresses pride in his son when he says, "This is my Son, the Beloved, with whom I am well pleased." That is God proudly presenting his son. He is looking down, beaming with pride, saying, "That's my boy!" And only men can pass down that kind of feeling to other men. Men need that same kind of love from their fathers. Brothers need it from brothers. We need it from one another. This is why nurturing is vital to our communities. If fathers aren't around, then young men should be able to bond with another man in their lives.

There are three reasons that males need this kind of emotional expression that can be described symbolically as "kissing on the neck." First, they need it because it helps a boy in his transition to becoming a man. There are a lot of men in pain and who are hurting in relationships because they did not have a father who nurtured them, who kissed them on the neck, and who taught them how to handle and express their emotions. A lot of men cannot achieve emotional intimacy because those tender and loving feelings were never truly developed within them. And when they feel those emotions welling up inside, they don't know what to do with them and how to properly express them. Men shut down and distance themselves rather than understanding that it is all right to be close and emotionally connected to another person. We then see men adopt a "cocoon mentality," whereby they shut down and distance themselves emotionally because it is a form of self-defense, a defense mechanism. In this psychological state, black men hide their compassionate side and flee from emotional bonding with others.

There are a lot of boys, emotionally speaking, who are trapped in men's bodies. They have a man's age, but emotionally, they have not grown up. They do not know how to talk to their wives. They do not know how to engage in a conversation and share the small things that make a marriage and family relationship special. A sort of "hand to hand combat" is the only kind of intimacy that some men understand. But marriage is not a battlefield. Young males need a father or some other significant male to help them transition emotionally from boyhood to manhood. Some of our fathers were too afraid to nurture us in that way. They wanted us to be tough, because life is tough. They did not want us to have a gentle side, as they believed that toughness signifies manliness. Too many men have been taught how to be good providers, but they are emotionally cold and distant. But gentleness is not weakness; gentleness is strength. Even God is a "gentle" man because gentleness is the restraint of force. Gentleness is strength. And real strength makes a boy a man.

Second, men need this experience of being "kissed on the neck" so that we can have a model of forgiveness. Men carry pent-up frustrations and anger that are rooted in an inability to forgive. They do not know how to express forgiveness because they never had a significant male in their life who modeled what it is like to forgive. Our young males are shooting each other in the streets like dogs because they are trying to settle the slightest argument with a gun rather than with forgiveness and love. They practice getting even where violence escalates—first the fist, then the knife, then the gun. All of us have transitioned through the phases of violent expression that have become the trademarks of our lives as African American men. What we need, now, is to learn how to express forgiveness.

The prodigal's father could have had any number of other responses to his son. He did not have to slam down the evening copy of the *Jerusalem Times,* jump out of his rocking chair, and take off running down that dusty road to embrace his son. He could have ignored the boy. He could have taken part in one of those petty games we like to play and said to himself, "Here he comes. What does he want now? He's spent all of the money, and now he's coming home." He could have said to his son, "What are you coming back here for, boy?" But this son had a father who knew how to forgive. He did not care if his son had blown the money. He just said, "I forgive you."

Third, we need to be "kissed on the neck" in order to know what it is like to be able to make a long-term commitment. Too many men go into a marriage promising to "try" to stay married. And, unfortunately, too many women have come to be satisfied with that. But, that is only because these same men do not know how to be in a long-term, committed relationship. Love will last a little while. But when the sweet strains of the violins in the background stop playing and the honeymoon is over, then the husband and wife have to make it on commitment. They have to say to one another, "Come hell or high water, I will be there for you." That is "kissing on the neck." And the "kissing on the neck" experience requires a long-term commitment.

The prodigal's father was committed to his son. He said, in effect, "Boy, I'm your father all of your life. You're my son all of my life. Even if you did run away and take your inheritance with you and waste it all, you've come back. You're still my son, and you're going to be my son until time ends. Period." That is a long-term commitment.

But what about men who did not have that "kissing on the neck" experience? Then, brothers, receive the love that is offered to you now. Go on and open up on the inside; receive the emotional support that someone is trying to give to you. It is all right, it is manly, it is healthy to feel those emotions that are stirring within you. Then, take the next step and risk loving. Take a chance on making that emotional bond and that loving commitment. Risk it all for the sake of having that "kissing on the neck" encounter.

Finally, return to the Father and let him "kiss you on the neck." That is what the prodigal son did. He was down there on the ground, sipping soup out of a pig's trough. He got tired of that. The boy remembered that he had been loved. And when you have been loved, you always know you can go back. Something inside of him told this boy that his father would often stand on the porch looking out over the distance just to see if his son was coming home. The son started to recall memories of home.

After a while, his wants, needs, and the misery of his condition got the best of him. He came to himself. He said, "I messed up. I've got the stench of the pigpen on me, but I'm getting up from here. I'm going back to my father's house." He returned to an embrace and a kiss on the neck, a father's kiss.

If you are a brother who does not have a biological father to return to, then I know a Father; his name is Jehovah. He became your father when Jesus became your savior and big brother. For Jesus said that he taught his disciples how to pray "Our Father who art in heaven...." Jesus did not simply say, "Father." He said, "*Our* Father."

And, brothers, all of you have a Father who loves you. You have a Father who cares about you. He will free you up for love and free you to be a man. If you have wandered far away from home, you can come home. The prodigal came back saying, "Make me a servant. Make me act as I should. Make me yours." And he was greeted with love and a kiss on the neck. God, our Father, will forgive you. He will welcome you with a Father's kiss.

chapter six
raising ANOTHER man's baby
c. dexter wise III

When Joseph awoke from sleep, he did as the angel of the
Lord commanded him; he took her as his wife, but had no
marital relations with her until she had borne a son; and he
named him Jesus. (Matthew 1:24–25, NRSV)

∞

before they came together

The wedding date had already been set. The local preacher had
already been secured. The sanctuary of the church had already
been scheduled. The reception hall had already been reserved. The
bridal gown had already been picked out. The engagement rings
were already on. Joseph and Mary were betrothed and set to get
married. As far as they could see or foresee, their marriage was just
a matter of time. There was nothing that either one of them could
"conceive" that might dampen their delight, alter their anticipation, or sabotage their celebration. However, the Bible tells us that
something *did* happen "before they came together."

"Before they came together" was the period between "Will
you?" and "I will." "Before they came together" was the time
between their agreement to spend the rest of their lives with
each other and their first sexual relation. In other words,
"before they came together" was the period between commitment and consummation.

As we peruse this passage, pay attention to a couple of points
about "before they came together." First, notice about this period that Mary and Joseph did not put consummation in front of

commitment. They did not attempt to get together sexually until they had made a legal and communal commitment publicly. These days, we have it backwards. We consummate first and think about commitment later, only to discover that, when we consummate without prior commitment, we often end up with only a little momentary pleasure instead of a lifetime marital partner.

Then, my black brothers, please don't fail to miss something else about "before they came together." That is, if something is wrong or going to go wrong with your relationship, it is always better to know about it before you come together. So much of what is out of order in marriages today has to do with unacknowledged or unaddressed conflicts, conditions, circumstances, and concerns that existed before they came together. Trust me, my brothers, no matter how painful it may be, if a bombshell is going to be dropped on your relationship, it is better to have it go off before you come together.

she was found to be with child

According to the text, Mary was found to be with child. It never tells us how she was found to be with child. Yet, from the way it reads, there is a good chance that she didn't just bring it up to Joseph. There is no suggestion that she volunteered the information. There is no hint that she deliberately disclosed her condition. Apparently, it came up at a time that she did not intend. It came out in a manner that she did not control. She was found to be with child.

When Mary was found to be with child, Joseph found himself in an uncomfortable, but not uncommon, predicament. In many ways, his problem was not unique. For, whenever one person commits to marry another person, the one they choose may not be with child, but they certainly are with something! They are with debt, with sickness, with scars, with issues, with disease, with hang-ups, with baggage, with in-laws, or with idiotic idio-syncrasies. Whenever you marry someone, no matter how perfect they appear or how sweet they sound, watch out, because they are always with something!

Beyond this general similarity, Joseph's predicament is common today because there are at least four irrefutable realties that make it more likely that, whenever a man finds a single woman of marrying age, she is already with child. The first of these irrefutable realities is teenage pregnancy. The good news is that the rate of teenage pregnancy is falling. The bad news is that the rate of teenage pregnancy is still alarmingly high. Young women come to biological maturity as early as nine years of age, but they don't come to emotional maturity until much later. This means that many of them have already experimented with sex and have had a baby long before they are ready to have and handle a husband. Thus, by the time they are old enough and mature enough to get married, they are already with child.

A second irrefutable reality of our time is closely connected with the first. It is the reality of teenage fathers and deadbeat dads. The young men with whom the aforementioned young women are having sexual relations are often at least as immature and irresponsible as their female counterparts. They, too, are biologically ready, but not emotionally or economically ready to be fathers or husbands. Many such fathers of all ages prove their unreadiness by cutting off communication with their child's mother and literally doing a Houdini, while everyone knows "who done it."

A third irrefutable reality that contributes to the large pool of single women with children is divorce. Families get started with honorable and great intentions. Nevertheless, marriages do collapse and, more often than not, the woman in the relationship has custody of the children. Now, this woman may be divorced, but she is not an old maid. Some of her dreams may have been dashed, but all of her desires have not been extinguished. She is still in her prime. She may still hope to share her life with a man. However, now she has three, four, or five children to bring into the equation. Therefore, whenever a man discovers her, he may find her to be witty and wonderful, but he will also find her to be with child.

The fourth irrefutable reality that makes Joseph's predicament quite common in our culture is the double standard for men and women as it relates to their children. The difference is that, for the most part, men "have child" and women are "with child." When a man fathers a child, the woman has the baby and, unfortunately, some men choose to freely go about their business. This leaves the woman with the child. When the man who already has a child by another woman chooses to marry a second woman, even though he has a child, he is not with the child. Therefore, his child is not the same kind of "package deal" as it would be for his child's mother. This man's second woman (or wife) only has to deal with the existence of a child. On the other hand, when a woman has a baby and is no longer with the baby's father, she is left by herself with the child. Then, any man who is interested in her must not only accept the existence of the child, but the regular presence of the child as well. So you see, my brothers, Joseph's predicament was uncomfortable, but actually was not that uncommon.

the child was of the holy ghost

Not only are we told that Mary was found with child, but we are also informed that this child was of the Holy Ghost. We know from the text that the child whom Mary carried was literally conceived in her by the Holy Ghost. He was the Son of God. His name was to be called Jesus because he would save his people from their sins.

Still, even this situation need not be considered completely unique. For it could be argued that, even if we find ourselves confronted with the birth of a baby under less than optimal circumstances, that child too might be of the Holy Ghost! Who knows what God is doing or might do through the life of this child? This is why we must learn to separate the parents' predicament from the child's possibilities.

I know some preachers who will not dedicate, in the church's sanctuary, a baby who has been born out of wedlock, but I have a problem with this. Why penalize the baby for grown folks' mess? Every child has a right to be brought before the altar and given back to God, regardless of the circumstances that brought him or her into the world. The mommy and daddy might be the devil personified, but who knows, maybe the child will be the first one in the family to follow Christ and lead the rest of them to the Lord! (As an aside, it is entirely possible for married people to have children out of wedlock. Just because you have a marriage license doesn't mean you are in wedlock. Millions of couples are technically married, but they are not speaking to each other. They sleep in separate beds. They live separate lives. They can't stand each other. Where is the wedlock? What they have is more like "wed loose" than wedlock!)

You never know who you are lifting up when you dedicate a child to God. Every child has a purpose, if none other than to draw its parents before God at the altar. In the case of Jesus, as in so many other cases, the child was born in confusion, but he was of the Holy Ghost! The child was born in controversy, but he was of the Holy Ghost. The child was born under a cloud, but he was of the Holy Ghost.

joseph thought about these things

Needless to say, when Joseph found out that Mary was with child, he had something to think about! He thought about the public perception. What would people say about Mary? She was an unwed teenager, pregnant with an unidentified man's child. What names would they call her? What treatment would they give her? Perhaps Joseph also wondered what people would say about him. Would they call him a chump? Might they call him a fool for letting this woman do this to him and then staying with her?

Furthermore, Joseph must have thought about how the public would perceive the child. What would they say about Jesus? They do have names for children who are born out of wedlock, you know! Even to the day that Jesus died, there must have been people in Nazareth who publicly called Jesus Joseph's son, but privately whispered, "Nobody knows who his real daddy is!"

Added to Joseph's thoughts about the public perception was the very fact of his love for Mary. This whole matter would have been infinitely easier if he didn't love her. According to Jewish law and practice, he had a right to embarrass her. He had a right to shame her. He had a right to divorce her. He even had a right to stone her. Joseph's problem was that he was committed to Mary and he loved her. Brothers, have you ever loved anybody who, when they do trifling things and stupid stuff, you want to put your hands around their throats and choke them? Yet, it's not the fear of the police that keeps you from doing it. It's not the terror of the electric chair that restrains you. It's your love that won't let you do it. Joseph had to think about the tension between his legal rights and his irresistible love.

While Joseph meditated on his situation, there is no doubt that he also thought about the prospect of having to compete with an invisible father. Whenever a man marries a woman with child, the biological father, although never physically present, is always there. The father may never be physically there, but, in some form or another, he is always there. The father may be invisible, but he is always there in the child's genes and in the child's dreams. He has his daddy's blood, his daddy's DNA, and even his daddy's looks. Furthermore, as the child grows, he will undoubtedly wonder at some point about his daddy. Where is he? Why did he leave? Does he love me? Should I go find him? Would my life have been better with my biological father than with this man that my mother married?

Beyond this, the biological father may be invisible, but he is always there in the mother's memories. No matter how much she denies it by saying, "That was years ago. That is over. I have no feelings for him," there is no way in the world a woman can love a child and completely forget the man who gave the child to her.

If this is not enough, the biological father might be invisible, but he is always present in Joseph's imagination. Behind every knock at the door, behind every envelope delivered by mail, and behind every ring of the telephone are the words "What if...?" What if she decides she wants to go back to the man who is the father of the baby after I have stepped into his responsibility? What if the baby grows up and decides that I am not good enough to be his daddy? What if, after being gone for fifteen years, the biological father develops a guilty conscience, shows up on my doorstep, and announces that he now wants to be a part of the child's life?

Joseph's competition with an invisible father is compounded by the fact that Jesus' father was not flesh and blood. It is bad enough to compete with an invisible father who is always there, but what about an invisible father who is everywhere? How can a man compete with the father of his wife's child if that father is the Holy Ghost? If ever there was a legitimate case of a "ghost dad," here it is!

how to raise another man's baby

Brothers, put yourself in Joseph's place. He was engaged to a woman who, at the last minute, turned out to be pregnant. What's a brother to do? How can a self-respecting man raise another man's baby, especially under such questionable circumstances? Well, Joseph gives us some help on how.

The first thing to mention is not what Joseph did, but what he was. Joseph was able to raise another man's baby because he was a just man (see Matthew 1:19). He wanted to do what was right. He had principles. He had values. He had ethics. He was righteous. Some women are looking for "just a man," not a "just man." However, there is a difference. "Just a man" will pursue you until he catches you. A "just man" will provide for you until he pleases you. "Just a man" will spend the night and wow you. A "just man" will spend his whole life working for you. "Just a man" will do whatever he wants. A "just man" will do whatever is right.

Next, as verse 24 shows, Joseph was able to raise another man's baby by not overreacting and by thinking first. It is obvious that Joseph thought first and did not overreact. If he had allowed his African roots to rise up immediately right after the Bible said that Mary was found with child, we would have read: "Then her husband Joe broke somebody's jaw, tore up somebody's tent, blackened somebody's eye, and went to jail!" "Come on," Joseph might have said, "You mean to tell me that you are pregnant and the best you can come up with is that the Holy Ghost did it? Don't insult my intelligence. My momma didn't raise no fool!" But Joseph didn't overreact. He thought first.

Many of the issues that arise between a father and his stepchild might also arise between a father and his natural child. Think first and don't overreact. African American brothers, we must let cool heads rather than hot heads prevail. I am convinced that this tendency to think and not overreact was a part of Joseph's nature. Remember when Jesus was lost in Jerusalem and stayed there for three days? After they finally found him, Mary asked Jesus why he would treat them like that and make them worry about him. And, with Joseph standing right there, Jesus said, "Mother, didn't you know that I must be about my Father's business?" Jesus wasn't talking about the carpentry business, either. Yet, we have no recorded reaction from Joseph. He had good cause to shout, "Look, boy, I have taken care of you and your mother for all these years and now you say you want to go about your father's business. Well, I tell you what, you go right ahead and let your father take care of you because I am not the one!" Instead, we hear nothing but silence from Joseph. He did not overreact. He didn't say anything to Jesus. He thought first. My take on it is that, after hearing Jesus' remark, Joseph turned to his wife and said through his teeth, "Mary, I'm walking ahead with the camels. *You* had better handle this!"

Then, Joseph was able to raise another man's baby by waiting on a word from the Lord. He didn't do anything until he heard from the Lord. In fact, all he did was think until he heard. And he did hear from God in a dream. He heard the Lord tell him what to do. Black men, don't assume that you know what to do. Seek the Lord's guidance and don't move until he gives the "Go!" sign. "Trust in the LORD with all your heart, and do not rely on your own insight. In all your ways acknowledge him, and he will make straight your paths" (Proverbs 3: 5–6).

Furthermore, Joseph shows us how to raise another man's baby by obeying the Lord with all of his heart. Once he heard the word, Joseph started walking and stopped worrying. He did as the angel of the Lord had bidden him. Once God puts his stamp on a situation, you can walk on without worry. Joseph could now say, "I didn't have anything to do with the baby coming here, but I am going to have everything to do with the baby staying here!"

Listen, brothers! Raising your own baby is your duty, but raising another man's baby is your privilege. Because you love the mother and the child, it is your privilege to help mold the life of someone who was not cared for. It is your privilege to breathe love into the life of someone who might otherwise go astray. It is your privilege to share in the life of someone who might ultimately change the world.

Now, you might reply to this, "Joseph got Jesus, but my girl's child is more like 'little Lucifer!'" To this, I must add that, when your little Lucifer comes into contact with a man of God, he will straighten up. When he sees a real man who stands on the principles of God, either the devil is going to get out of him or he is at least going to act like an angel in your presence. Don't you allow your little Lucifer to turn you into a "big Lucifer." Instead, study with him. Mentor him. Share with him. Encourage him. Bless him. Pray with him. Play with him. Be there for him. Most of all, love him.

the bottom line

Some of you say you can't relate to this because you've never had to raise another man's baby. However, whether you realize it or not, every child that you raise belongs to another man. Your child belongs to God, and you will be held accountable by the baby's Father for how you treat that child.

Other brothers may ask, "Why should I raise another man's baby?" The answer that comes to you does not come from me, but from the Lord. He says, "You should raise another man's baby because I raised you! Your father may have planted, your mother may have watered you, but I gave the increase! I raised you from the projects and turned you into one of my pet projects. I raised you from a sense of shame and gave you godly pride. I raised you from depending on your momma to depending on me. I raised you from a crowd that was on their way to death and destruction to a people who are on their way to a great coronation. I raised you from the shadow of death in foxholes, rice patties, and back allies to abundant and everlasting life. I raised you from one graduation to another. I raised you from being an employee to being an employer. I raised you from 'I can't do it' to 'I can do all things through Christ!' I raised you from a boy with no identifiable earthly father to a man with an unconditional heavenly father. When your father and mother forsook you, I took you up. When everybody else put you down, I picked you up. When your so-called friends put you out, I stepped in."

"The bottom line," says the Lord, "is: The reason you ought to raise another man's baby is the undeniable love you have for the baby's mother and the unconditional love I have shown in raising you!"

My brothers, in this global village, we are all responsible for one another. As we ponder how God has taken care of us, let us find ways to take care of others.

chapter seven

daddy's little GIRL: finding the miracle in your nightmare

otis moss III

Then Amnon said to Tamar, "Bring the food into the chamber, so that I may eat from your hand." So Tamar took the cakes she had made, and brought them into the chamber to Amnon her brother. But when she brought them near him to eat, he took hold of her, and said to her, "Come, lie with me, my sister." She answered him, "No, my brother, do not force me; for such a thing is not done in Israel; do not do anything so vile! As for me, where could I carry my shame? And as for you, you would be as one of the scoundrels in Israel. Now therefore, I beg you, speak to the king; for he will not withhold me from you." (2 Samuel 13:10–13, NRSV)

∞

if, according to theologian dwight hopkins, Jesus is the sum total of our liberation quest, then all human issues of suffering should be explored, demystified, confronted, engaged, and placed within the context of Christ. My brothers in Christ, I solicit your prayers as we embark upon dangerous territory by exploring a difficult text and a painful subject matter.

I bring to your attention, under the guidance of the Holy Spirit, the portrait of a family and the pain of a young woman named Tamar, a woman whose name is associated with the palm trees of northern Africa, a tree that brings forth fruit and promise. Tamar, I believe, was a woman of promise whose life was shattered by a despicable act. Biblical scholars, except a few feminist theologians, have skipped over Tamar's life because one critical moment in her history banished her from the homiletical hierarchy of canonized characters lifted up by purveyors of the Word. Tamar—a woman of promise, a woman of potential, a woman of possibility, a woman of purpose, and a woman of poise—has been placed so far upon the margin by the church that her name does not appear upon the scroll of any theological dialogue, hermeneutical inquiry, or exegetical investigation performed by the community of faith. She sits, my brothers, in a forgotten abyss—somewhere north of Job's suffering and east of Jeremiah's tears—with her head bowed and arms clutching her own frail, female frame, muttering through her tears, "Why? Why?"

I, as resident theologian of this small body of believers, want to apologize to you, Tamar, for all timid preachers, uneasy laypersons, oppressive scholars, and ignorant historians. Tamar, we are sorry! Sorry we did not tell your story. Sorry our children are ignorant of your pain. Sorry we did not cry tears with you. Sorry we were scared to tell your story for fear the mythical overseers of church etiquette would reprimand our conduct. Sorry we did not tell the truth about what happened in the king's palace. Maybe one day you can forgive us for hiding you between David's indiscretion and Absalom's violent death.

Tamar's story begins in the hallowed halls of the royal family of Israel. David, the king and anointed of God, has been blessed with male children, but this father has yet to feel the joy of having a little girl. Through the womb of Maacah, a "woman child" is born. She is bestowed the name Tamar. Her name will mean "palm tree with the promise of fruit." David, I imagine, was excited about his boys, but this little girl, his only girl, must have captured his heart. Little Tamar was the princess of the palace and, rightly so, for her father was the king. She was royalty under the protection of Daddy. This little girl was filled with wonder and joy as she experienced life as a girl of privilege and promise.

What gave this girl her greatest joy was knowing that she was Daddy's little girl!

The relationship between a parent and child is sacred. A soul, wrapped in human flesh, created in the image of God, is placed in the frail hands of women and men. Children are God's gift to humanity. It is through a child, not a man but a small piece of human flesh birthed from Mary's womb, that salvation comes. Children are a gift from God, and we are required to love, teach, and encourage them. The relationship between a mother and child is sacred, but the relationship between a father and child carries special responsibility. When a man becomes a father, his little girl will learn from him what to accept and reject in a relationship. Sisters and brothers caught in the destructive cycle of domestic abuse often witness a father, uncle, or friend as the prototype of this behavior. We need men, brothers, who are unafraid to love their girls and boys. We need men who are unashamed to bow down and pray. We need men who will have the courage to ask for forgiveness. We need men who want to be more than "baby's daddies," "players," "ballers," and "shot callers."

I just want to raise the question, "Are there any black men who are willing to repair broken relationships, to seek out estranged children and ask them for forgiveness, to love their wives, to stop being 'rolling stones' and to become stable men able to pray unto God?" Brothers, God does not care what mistakes you have made in the past. Our community is crying out right now; we are looking for good men, not perfect men, but good men! We are looking for men who will, as singer Donnie McClurkin says, stand back up after they fall down. Brothers, you can get up and reclaim the sacred gift of fatherhood!

Our relationship with our daughters is sacred. A girl should have a relationship with a man, as she develops, who wants nothing from her sexually. She needs the love of both a mama and a daddy but, in our community, fathers are desperately needed. I speak not of biology, for biology only makes a baby; but only a man of honor can become a father. Men of honor are needed to lay a foundation of Christ-centered love where girls can become women in a nonviolent and loving home. We have, unfortunately, placed childrearing solely on the shoulders of our sisters but, brothers, it is time for us to "flip the script" and protect our Tamars and prosecute our Amnons.

What is so tragic about this text is that the violation upon Tamar is not caused by a stranger but by someone she knew! The people involved did not pull her down a back alley. She knew the culprit. It was her brother! She was hurt at home! Home should be a place of protection, a place of direction, and a place for our consecration into maturity. Home is designed to be our hope in ages past and a shelter from our stormy blasts. But it is also in this place of alleged comfort and security where we receive our deepest wounds. It is from those we love and with whom we share the same roof that the greatest pain is potentially inflicted. Nothing hurts like being hurt at home. Tamar, I can only imagine your pain, shame, anger, guilt, rage, confusion, and fear.

But the text also gives a prophetic word to this vile situation. The text shows that it was not her fault. Tamar did not cause this situation; she did not ask for it. Beyond all the foolish rhetoric preached by foolish men, it is seldom the fault of the violated when they are violated. I am here to proclaim this day, It was not your fault, Tamar! I care not what you were told or what you believe—it was not your fault!

Some of us who gather behind the sacred walls of the church can identify with the rage of Tamar. This woman was abused and violated in a place which was to be a refuge. If I am not safe at home, where am I safe? This kind of violation is already horrific, but what makes it unbearable is that Daddy did not protect his little girl. She was David's only girl, but he refused to punish Amnon for the crime he committed against his baby girl. David,

I believe, did not want a public scandal in his court. He sought to keep this immoral act on the "DL," the down low. As a result of David's cowardice, Tamar was violated twice—once by her brother and now by the inaction of her father. More black men need to understand that passive-aggressiveness is detrimental to all aspects of our relationships with our daughters. Passive-aggressiveness is inaction, and no action is still action; it sends a message to others, in this case, Tamar and Amnon.

Tamar is not a one-dimensional victim, but rather a woman of defiance; she refuses to just be a victim suffering in silence. She makes a bold decision to put on sackcloth and ashes. This ritual, performed by the Hebrews, signified a great distress and sorrow upon the soul of a person. It was a public display of anguish. Tamar put on sackcloth and ashes and symbolically told David, Amnon, and all of Israel that something was wrong in the palace; Daddy's little girl has traded her royal robes for sackcloth. She had the courage to let everybody know that, although she was the princess of the palace, she had issues. Black men, what are our little girls trying to tell us today? What are our little boys trying to convey to us in their attitudes? What are our wives trying to tell us with their tears? Brothers, what are we trying to tell each other when we fight each other?

It is time that we, my brothers, learn from Tamar! We must put on our sackcloth and ashes! Too often, we come to church acting as if we are the prince and the princess, but behind our suit and Tommy Hilfiger jeans, all is not right in the palace! But this place we call church is the place to put on our sackcloth and ashes. We come to this place not because we've got it all together, but because there are problems only Jesus can solve. If you dare to come to church wrapped in sackcloth and ashes, you will find that you are not alone. You are not the only man who has been violated. You are not the only man who was addicted. You are not the only man whose marriage almost fell apart. You are not the only man who has been through a divorce. You are not the only man trying to raise three children on one income. Bring your sackcloth and ashes to the church as we take everything as a church to God in prayer. There is power in numbers. The demonic force of depression cannot live in collective praying company!

Sackcloth and ashes suggest that people in pain know where to go when they need release from their pain. As people of color in the Antebellum South, we knew how to put on sackcloth and ashes and cry out to God. We sang "Sometimes, I Feel Like a Motherless Child" in sackcloth and ashes. We sang "I Want Jesus to Walk with Me" in sackcloth and ashes. We cried out when we were in trouble to a Savior who hears the songs of a violated people. The sackcloth and ashes were invitations to and for Jesus to enter into our soul-shattering predicaments. Black men, we need to adorn ourselves with sackcloth and ashes, and we need to invite Jesus into our lives, regardless of the situation.

But after we sang the songs in sackcloth and ashes, we also knew how to change clothes and move beyond our pain. It was in the worship experience that our anguish was transformed to "amens," and our pain was translated to praise. As a people, we know about pain, but we also know about praise. We know about violation, but we also know about victory. It is OK to wear your sackcloth. Wear it, my brothers, but make sure that you have a change of clothes.

Tamar never took off her sackcloth and ashes, which means that the rest of her life was defined by the violation. There will come a time, brothers, when you will have to move beyond your violation, beyond your tears, beyond your heartbreak, beyond your midnight, and get up in the morning and put on new clothes. Do not become defined or consumed by your past. I know that your divorce hurt, but you were a child of God before the divorce, as you will be after the divorce. I know that your conviction hurt, but you were made in his image before you were locked up, and you are still a reflection of his grace afterwards. I know that it hurt when she walked out on you, but you are still breathing, even though you are still "Waiting to Exhale." We must change our clothes!

Let me see if I can break this down for you. As a young boy, I idolized my big sister Daphne. She was the genius of the family. Sister girl was tough! She introduced me to Maya Angelou, Langston Hughes, Zora Neal Hurston, James Baldwin, and others. My sister was tough, I tell you. When she went off to college, she fell in love with some brother and came home the next summer talking about her boyfriend. I was happy for her because she was happy. This was my sister, my ace, and I was thrilled because she was thrilled.

One year later, she came home for the summer wearing sackcloth and ashes. Brother man had broken her heart. I was ten at the time and ready to hurt somebody for hurting my sister! Daphne said, "Otis, don't worry, I will be all right." She did not look all right and was not acting all right, but I listened and chilled out.

She kept her sackcloth and ashes of heartbreak on all summer, until the week before school was to start. All of a sudden, she changed clothes. She was not moping around the house looking like Job. I said, "Daphne, what happened?" She said, "I found a miracle in this nightmare. The Lord spoke to me through a song." "A song?" I repeated. "What kind of song?" "A disco song!" she replied. I knew my sister was losing it. "The Lord does not speak through disco songs, Sis." Her reply: "Well, he did for me. I was listening to the radio and this old song by Gloria Gaynor came on, 'I Will Survive.' Otis, I know I will survive!"

My brothers, I want to tell you that, no matter what you have been through, you will survive! You are still here! You made it through "every danger, toil, and snare" and you survived. Why? Because our Savior empowers us, the Holy Ghost covers us, and the Father clothes us! You made it through every storm and you survived. Why? Because a man born in a manger provided you with the spiritual survival skills called the fruits of the Spirit: love, joy, peace, patience, kindness, generosity, faithfulness, gentleness, and self-control (see Galatians 5:22). Against such things, there is no law, no weapon, no violation that can destroy you!

You made it through every dark season and you survived. Survival is based on our present relationship with Christ, not our past predicament. It is time to change clothes, to put away the sackcloth and ashes, and to put on the full armor of God! For our struggle is not against flesh and blood, but against the rulers, against authorities, against powers of this dark world, and against spiritual forces of evil in the heavenly realms! Put on the full armor of God and find the miracle lurking in your nightmare!

chapter eight
why, daddy, WHY?
c. dexter wise III

At three o'clock Jesus cried out with a loud voice, "Eloi, Eloi, lema sabachthani?" which means, "My God, my God, why have you forsaken me?" (Mark 15:34, NRSV)

∞

it's a funny thing about children: you get what you pray for! You pray for them. You pray about them. Then, when God answers your prayers, you are sorry! You pray to have a child. Then you conceive, are sick the whole time, and you are sorry. You pray that the child will finally come out of the womb. Then, when your lady's water breaks, the labor begins and you are sorry. You pray that the baby will start sleeping through the night. Now the baby is up all day and you're sorry. You pray that the baby will learn how to feed itself; then, she starts eating objects other than food, and you're sorry. You pray that the baby learns to walk; then he wants to walk down steps, into your kitchen cabinets, play in the toilet, and you are sorry. You pray that your child learns how to talk; then she begins to talk and spout out speech which drives you crazy, and you are sorry.

Babies quickly learn three expressions that every parent knows. The first such expression (which drives mothers crazy the most) is "Dada." Here, the mother, at two o'clock in the morning, is feeding the baby, taking care of the baby, nursing the baby, changing the baby, and the first thing that comes out of the baby's mouth is not "Mama" but "Dada." A second expression that babies utter almost as soon as they learn to talk is "No!" They hit those terrible twos and, if you're not careful, you'll end up hit-ting them because all they can say is "No!" For a while it seems like "no!" is the only word they know. But, then, I've discovered that it doesn't take long for babies who have learned how to talk to begin to shout one more expression. It is only one syllable, but what a powerful word it is. The word is neither "Dada" or "No!" Every baby, sooner or later, will ask "Why?"

If there is anything that will drive you crazy, it's little children asking "Why?" There are no questions like a child's questions. They are innocent questions. They are sincere questions. They are profound questions. These children are like two-foot-tall philoso-phers who ask "Why?" "Daddy, why is the sky blue?" "Daddy, why do men and women have to go into different bathrooms?" "Daddy, why was I born and how did I get here?" "Daddy, why did that man call you 'boy'?" "Daddy, why did my doggie die, and where did he go when he died?"

Most parents don't have sense enough to simply tell their chil-dren, "I don't know!" So they give them one of three standard parental answers to the question "Why, Daddy, why?" First you try "Because that's just the way it is." If that doesn't work, you blurt out, "Because I said so!" And if your child is still unsatis-fied, then you tell them, "Go ask your mother!"

Most of us are quite grown. We are no longer children. Yet we still have some questions that we would like to ask our daddies. If you could ask your daddy any question you wanted to, with-out being worried about a whipping, what would it be? If he is dead and you could raise him from the dead, what would you ask him? If he has disappeared and you could find him, what would you ask him? If he is alive and well and you could call him, what would you ask him? These often suppressed interrogatives are not the product of inquiring minds that want to know; they are the cries of hurting hearts that need to be healed. "Daddy, why don't I look like you?" "Daddy, why is my last name different from yours?" "Daddy, why can't you stay with us all the time?" "Daddy, why can't you and Mommy be happy?" "Daddy, remember when you went away and stayed away for a month, where did you go?" "Daddy, why have you forsaken me?"

I wonder if there are any men reading this chapter who've felt forsaken by their daddy. Is there a male reading this chapter whose daddy has denied you? Disappeared on you? Despised you? Deceived you? Disowned you? Dispossessed you? Divorced you? Disappointed you? Deserted you? Or just up and died on you? Is there any man reading this essay who has felt forsaken by his father?

Well, my brethren, if you have ever felt like a forsaken child, you are not alone because Mark 15 tells us that the world's most famous son of the world's most famous Father felt what you and I have felt. That is, he felt forsaken by his father. And just like us, Jesus asked, "Why, Daddy, why?"

Up to the point of his suffering on the cross of Calvary, Jesus never questioned his father. In fact, Jesus seldom even addressed his father in the interrogative mood. He spoke in the indicative. He spoke in the imperative. He spoke in the declarative. He spoke in the subjunctive. However, Jesus hardly ever spoke to his father in the interrogative—until Calvary.

It's not that asking God a question never crossed Jesus' mind. It was only that, up to that point, Jesus had learned how to live with his questions and perhaps divert his attention every time it seemed like it might come to the surface. You know how we, especially men, can become extremely efficient in suppressing our deepest hurts and at artfully dodging the desire to ask our most burning questions. But when you are being nailed in your hands, pierced in your side, mocked and cursed for nothing you have done, trust me, a whole lot of stuff comes up! Being crucified or being in a crisis will force you to drop your façade and to finally ask what you really wanted to know all along.

This is exactly how it is for so many of us, my brothers. For too long, we have had so many questions we wanted to ask our daddies, but we've learned how to be functional in our dysfunctional situations. And if something comes up, we step on it and squash it because we don't want to deal with whatever the answer might be. Yet when you are being crucified, when you are being nailed to the cross, that little boy in you just has to know and shouts, "Why, Daddy, why?"

As we read Mark's account of the crucifixion with some degree of a sanctified imagination, we are able to enter into the holy hush of this hill. If we listen really carefully, then we might be able to hear some of the obvious but unuttered and unrecorded "Why, Daddy, why?" questions of Christ. Now imagine what Jesus might have asked his daddy as he hung on the cross.

Daddy, why do you say good things about me to other people in public, but not to me in public? Jesus might say, "Remember at my baptism, you didn't say, 'You've done a good job, boy!' You spoke to everybody else there but me. You said, 'This is my beloved son in whom I am well pleased.' Why didn't you say that to me, instead of to them? Then, it happened again on the mount of transfiguration. You told my disciples that I was your son, and that above Elijah and Moses they should hear me. While I am glad that you said that, why didn't you say it to me?" How many children have fathers who brag to everyone else about them, but never utter a single sound of praise directly to them? Why are men not free enough to praise their children? Why is it that men can be so proud and yet can't open their mouths and say, "I love you"? Why, Daddy, why?

Daddy, why is my mother here, but you are not? Jesus just might have remarked, "When I look around from the cross, it seems like I can't find you and yet Momma is right here. Why is it that I can depend on Momma, but when I look for you, I feel forsaken? My mother, Mary, bore the reproach of a whole nation simply in standing by the cross." Jesus could have easily asked, "Why is Momma here, but you are not?" Brothers, for those of us with the same question, it was Momma who took us to practice. It was Momma who took us to football games. It was Momma who took us to our graduation. It was Momma who took us to the hospital. It was Momma who took us to the barber shop. It was Momma who taught us how to drive. Why is it that Momma stuck with us and Daddy did not? She is supposed to be a part of the weaker sex, and yet in the times of most stress, we see Momma, but Daddy has forsaken us.

Daddy, why would you set Momma up to break her heart like this? She did not ask to become pregnant. She was happily engaged to Joseph, and you found her. You selected her. You overshadowed her, knowing all the time that this was going to happen to her. Why would you impregnate her, knowing that thirty-three years later, her son would have an appointment with a cross and that it was going to break her heart?" How many sons are there who look at their birth situations and know that Daddy didn't mean well from the beginning? They want to ask, "Why, Daddy, why?"

Daddy, why do I have to take care of my mother? That's not my job, that's your job! "You made absolutely no arrangements for her retirement or care in my absence. I had to interrupt my dying to take care of her. I said to her, 'Woman, behold thy son.' And then to John I said, 'Son, behold thy mother.'" How many other sons are resentful and angry about the fact that they could not just be a son but, instead, they had to be a husband to their mother and a father to their siblings in the absence of some man?

Daddy, why don't you say something? "I'm up here dying, I'm crying out for you, and all I hear is silence. I know you know how to talk. You spoke the world into existence. You spoke Moses out of a burning bush. You spoke through Balaam's donkey. Yet, when I need you the most, there is nothing but silence."

Someone else reading this chapter has also suffered from his father's silence. No card on your birthday. No call for Christmas. No letter to let you know that your father is even alive. No congratulations on your graduation. No money for your marriage. Nothing but silence. "Why, Daddy, why?"

Daddy, why have you, of all people, forsaken me? "I could take it when my own people forsook me. You know, I came unto my own and they received me not. I could handle it when hundreds of my followers fell away after they discovered what I was about. I was not even shocked when all of my closest disciples, including Peter, left me. But not you, too. I relied on you. I depended on you. I trusted you, and look what it got me. You could have stepped in and stopped all of this at any time, but you didn't. Daddy, why have you forsaken me?"

My brother, you must be thinking that I have almost gone over the edge of prophetic license and I'm on the borderline of blasphemy with this imagined line of questioning. However, since I've already started, permit me now to suggest how, indeed, God might have responded to such "Why, Daddy, why?" questions. God might have said:

Son, the reason you are going through what you are going through is because you are caught up in something that started before you were born. "Jesus, you came into the world because sin was here long before you got here. In fact, you came to save people from their sin. For other sons, there were also many things that were wrong before they were born and they are catching it now because of that. Circumstances were wrong. Relationships were wrong. Intentions were wrong. Commitments were wrong. My son, the reason you feel forsaken is because you are dealing with stuff that started long before you were born."

Son, you feel forsaken, but it's not your fault; it's mine. "Jesus, you wonder what you did to deserve this. Nothing! I decided that the only way to save a sinful world was to sacrifice a sinless life, and the only way to find a sinless life was to raise up one out of my own loins. You are not suffering because of any decision you made or any action you did. You are suffering because of what I, your father, decreed." Children often wonder, "What have I done to deserve this?" "If I had been a better child, would there have been more peace in my home?" "If I had gotten better grades, would Daddy still be with us?" "If I had never been born, would my parents be divorced?" My brothers, you must know that it's not you who is to blame. It's your father. You are innocent, but his guilt made him forsake you. His pride did not allow him to admit his mistakes. His fear wouldn't enable him to risk reaching out to you. His shame wouldn't allow him to own up to you. No! The problem is not you! It is in him!

Son, don't assume that because I seem absent from you that you are not present with me. God might argue: "Do you think it is easy for me to sit up here in glory and watch you die when I have the power to stop it? I can't bear to look. If I look, I'll stop it, and if I stop it, then the whole world will be lost." I'm sure that there are some dads who are no longer in the lives of their children who would say, "Don't you think I wanted to call? Don't you know I think about you every day? I wanted to come back. I wanted to speak. I wanted to help. I wanted to be a part of your life. But I didn't have the heart to and didn't know how to."

You are crying out to me after three hours of darkness, but when the light comes on, you will see that all the time I've been working behind the scenes, and it's going to be all right. "Jesus, my son, all the time that you were suffering, I was working out the salvation of the world. All the time that you were suffering, I was releasing the penalty of death. All the time that you were suffering, I was erasing the sins of humanity. All the time that you were suffering, I was getting ready to raise you up! Son of the African diaspora, you probably can't see it in your suffering, but I'm working things out."

The bottom line is that, in spite of the "Why, Daddy, why" questions of Christ, Jesus never received verbal response from God. There was only silence. Yet Jesus still said, "Father, into your hands I commend my spirit." Before Easter ever came, before the resurrection was a reality, before deliverance had been demonstrated, with the blood still flowing and with the pain still racking his body, Jesus said, "Father, into your hands…."

If nothing else, brothers, this teaches us a very important point: There are some questions you and I are going to have to live with until we get to glory. Yet you must trust God enough to be able to say, "Into your hands I commend my spirit."

I don't know about you, but I've got some "Why, Daddy, why" questions that I want to ask God. He is my Daddy. For I have been adopted and have been given permission to cry "Abba," which is Aramaic for "Daddy." I want to ask him, "Daddy, why do the wicked prosper?" "Daddy, why do you give the devil so much power?" "Daddy, why do the good die young?" "Daddy, why do children die hungry?" "Daddy, why does cancer kill so many people?" "Daddy, why does racism and prejudice still exist?" "Daddy, why do black men have to struggle so hard?" "Daddy, why do the heathen rage?" "Daddy, why do I have to cry sometimes?" "Daddy, why do I have to walk alone sometimes?" "Daddy, why are you taking so long to send Jesus back?" "Why, Daddy, why?"

Then, when I am at my wit's end, I hear from the pen of Charles Albert Tindley and the pages of the hymnal:

We will understand it better by and by.
By and by, when the morning comes,
When the saints of God are gathered home,
We'll tell the story how we've overcome,
For we'll understand it better by and by.

chapter nine

living single, but NOT alone

ralph douglas west

And Joseph's master took him and put him into the prison, the place where the king's prisoners were confined; he remained there in prison. But the LORD was with Joseph and showed him steadfast love; he gave him favor in the sight of the chief jailor. (Genesis 39:20–21, NRSV)

∞

where is god when you need him? it seems that when you need God, he can never be found. Where is God when you need him? Here I am, looking at a twenty-year stretch for a felony that I didn't commit. Twenty years to life is what I'm facing. The trumped-up charges brought against me by Potiphar's wife are called "aggravated sexual assault." I didn't lay my hands on that woman, and here I am, landed in this place with these hardened felons who once worked for Mr. Potiphar. I wonder how many of these fellows are on a stretch like mine for something they didn't do? Maybe this woman's MO is "If I can't have you, then I'll have you locked up."

What am I doing in Egypt in the first place? I never should have been here. How did it happen anyway? Oh, yeah, it's amazing how time makes you trace every single detail of your past. All I did was to put on that coat my father gave me. I can remember how proud he was when he hand-stitched it himself, placing different colors in it. The "multicolored coat" he called it, with sleeves the colors of leisure: green for growth, red for passion, and purple for loyalty. I can remember how he tailor-made that coat especially for me. I wish he wouldn't have asked me to wear it out in that field when he sent me to give my brothers that message.

There was something about the way they looked at me in that coat from a distance, how they watched me walk up to them. I heard them murmur, "Here comes that old dreamer." I wondered why they called me that when I hadn't told them any of my dreams at that time. I suppose they noticed something in me that I didn't recognize in myself. Maybe I'm really in an Egyptian prison cell because of the way my brothers felt about their step-mother, my beloved mama. It's days like these that I wish I could e-mail her, fax her. But all those privileges have been taken away from me here in jail. I just have to sit here and think about her.

I can remember how my father's face brightened, how his face lit up when he talked about his beloved Rachel, about her wonderful eyes and how warm they were, how sensual she looked when he met her at that well, and how he had to work overtime to marry her. When my father talked about her, it was always with such fond affection—"my beloved Rachel." Lord, my father loved that woman!

I'm not sure, but perhaps those brothers of mine became upset with me because my father often looked at me and said, "I sure am glad you look like your mother and not like me." Maybe that's why he made that coat; since he couldn't give her any more dowries, he added that coat to my collection. I can recall that day so clearly when my father told me to go to the fields with a message for my brothers. I saw big Reuben standing there with Judah, Simeon, Gad, Issachar, and Dan. I saw them out there working in the fields, and I saw a jaundiced look in their eyes as I walked up to them. It's amazing how you remember things like that when you're locked up in jail. I never paid any attention to that when I was in the free world, but now that I'm in here, I can tell that there was a smirk on Reuben's face. Even Judah's mouth was twisted. I can't figure that out for anything. That goes against the meaning of his name. My father told me that he was named "praise" because God had answered his prayer. But apparently he wasn't living up to his name. I can recall that day now that I've been here away from him long enough in time and distance.

Yes, I remember it all so well. I can see it as plainly as I can see the hand before my face. I remember how they began to mutter indistinguishably. Time has a way of taking away the cacophony of words, allowing me to hear what they were talking about. "Here comes that old dreamer," they said. Well, my brothers, I didn't create the dreams. They were given to me as a kind of divine intimation, some sort of "godly intervention." I'm not sure. I simply had a dream of a big light and some little lights. My father was wise enough to pick up on it. He told me, "Don't talk about it." But you know how it is—when you have a dream, you just have to tell somebody about it.

Before I realized it, I was in the field telling my brothers about this dream. I told them about a big sheaf and some smaller sheaves. They readily knew I was referring to myself as being higher than they were and their being subject to me. Without warning, they seized me, gagged and bound me, and dragged me through the dirty streets. They found an abandoned cistern in which to throw me. I'm certainly glad that thing was dry because, in hindsight, I believe those boys would have let me drown as they stood on the lip of that cistern, looking down in that black hole where I was bound and gagged, fighting for my life. While I struggled for air, they kicked dust down in the hole saying, "Let him die." But, thank God, somebody spoke up, allowing reason to rule over their faulty judgment. "We had better not kill him," they decided.

What they did was probably worse than death. They hated the coat. They took it, ripped it up, and killed an innocent goat. The poor thing was sacrificed for nothing. They probably threw its remains to the wind and put that goat's blood on the coat. They took it home to my father and said, "Daddy, look what some wild beast has done to your beloved Joseph."

I wonder how my father is doing now. I'm willing to bet that, with the death of Rachel and with my presumed death, he's inconsolable. I'm certain he moves about in constant bereavement. Knowing my father the way I do, I'm certain he's thinking, "If I had not been such a rascal when I was growing up, these things would never have befallen my children." I know he's wrestling with guilt. I wish I could tell him, "Daddy, you haven't done anything wrong; it's those brothers of mine."

Where is God when you need him? They sold me to a band of Midianites whose caravan passed by. Those fellows took care of me. But the way in which they disposed of me was so humiliating. They put me in the stock. There I stood naked, exposed, with everyone looking at me. I was sold to the highest bidder, while people whistled and threw coins at me. The shame was overwhelming. Where is God when you need him?

My father often talked about this God whom he had met in this little town called Luz. After he had seen angels going up and coming down on a heavenly ladder, he renamed the place Bethel, "the house of God." He often talked about how God and he walked together from that time on. But where is my father's God now? Where is he when you need him?

It's amazing how these prison stays make you think about everything. I remember that I ended up here in Egypt. Before I was incarcerated, Egypt was all right. It hurt me to be away from my family, but Egypt was tolerable—a new culture, new country, new language. I had to learn all this, so I exposed myself to it. I did a quick study on life at this "university" here, and I grew up fast. I met different kinds of people and, before I knew it, I was a favorite in this nation. Yet I dared not tell them about my father's God. This God was always with me.

Working for Potiphar was a rewarding experience, at first. He was chief over the Pharaoh's bodyguards, and I became his right-hand man. I had never engaged in hand-to-hand combat, nor was I skilled in body guarding, but there was something in me that he admired. "I like you, young man. I can work with you. I can trust you," he would say. "In fact, I like you so much that I'm going to make you my right-hand man. We think and act alike. I don't want you working out in the fields. Come work in my house."

I can remember that first day in Egypt when these things began to develop, and I spent weeks getting to know Potiphar. After some time, he took me to his house. I declare, I never saw a house like that before—those huge marble columns, that big veranda that wrapped all the way to the back, and the landscape sloped into the Nile River. I'd never seen so many servants. I was accustomed to wealth, but Egyptian money was more abundant than in Israel. My father owned herds of livestock, but the Egyptians owned diamonds, rubies, and emeralds.

I wish my story could end right there, but I knew from the moment those big doors swung open that something would happen. Potiphar was so happy walking me through the lobby of his house. We walked down stairways and turned corners, and we passed by busts of different gods lining the walls. We opened a large door to a spacious room, and I looked around at all of the furnishings. There was a sleek leopard skin chaise lounge in this room. I wish that was all that I had seen. I looked up and saw Potiphar's wife. She had a lovely face and body. She had style and charisma. To be sure, she looked nice, but I knew from my first day in that house, by the way she ogled me, that there would be trouble. It seemed like she peered right through me. I glanced around the room to see what she was looking at. She looked me up and down. I couldn't believe how bold she was. Potiphar was standing there, and she looked at me that way. I was so glad when Potiphar said, "Let's go out and let me show you some more of the house."

I wish the story ended there, but when you're in prison, you think about a lot of things. I knew that, since we hadn't known each other that long, he should have made me work my way into the house. But the opposite happened; Potiphar said, "Joseph, I'm putting you over everything I have. My only concern is the food I eat." I wanted so badly to say, "You have some other issues you need to be concerned about," but it wasn't my place to say it. Besides, he trusted me with the run of his house, with all the fiduciary responsibilities, including purchases and the negotiation of deals for the house.

The only thing I didn't like is summed up in a song my father listened to when he felt depressed. A guy by the name of Bobby Womack would sing something about wishing you wouldn't trust him so much. Now I know why, every now and then, my father listened to that song. When Potiphar gave me the run of his house, he started taking these overnight trips, being gone two to three days at a time. He often asked, "Joseph, do you need anything? Do you need anything to help you around the house?" "No, sir, everything is fine. In fact, why don't you let me stay outside?" I would ask. "No, you stay in here. If you want anything, just ask my wife for it; she'll get it for you." He didn't know how true that statement was.

Not long after that, it started. I could hear her comments periodically, then with regularity, day after day after day. "Joseph." She called me by my first name in a whisper so no one could hear her. "Joseph." The more I came into the house, the more she said, "Joseph." After a while, she started stretching out my name, "J-o-s-e-p-h." The way she greeted me when I'd come in the house was working on me.

When people hear about me in the future and read about my life, they may want to portray me as a man made of marble and stone. Not so. I was in my early twenties, a healthy, red-blooded young man, and this woman was doing this to me repeatedly. I was confused sometimes. Every day, it was, "Hi, Joseph." When she started in with her plan, she said, "Now, Joseph, you know my husband told you that, whatever I want, you must give it to me." But I replied, "I don't think he was talking about my assuming his role." "Who's going to know?" she asked. Then she said, "Joseph, you're one of the Hebrews, aren't you"? I responded, "Yes, ma'am." "Don't call me 'ma'am. I'm your age." "Yes, ma'am." "Joseph, I told you not to call me ma'am. It must be hot over there where you come from. You Hebrews have that beautiful dark tan." She always commented on my physique, how well built I was, and how sculptured my body was. She asked me to come in, go get this, retrieve that, to fetch this and that. I knew what she was doing, constantly watching me walk back and forth in front of her. It's amazing the things that you can remember when you're facing a stay that you don't deserve.

Then the day came. I remember this day as clearly as the day my brothers gagged me, bound me, and threw me in that cistern. It's amazing how trouble makes you remember certain days out of your life so well.

Cling, ling, ling. I came running into the house at the sound of her bell. "Yes, ma'am," I answered, bowing low. "Joseph," she said. I knew that this was the day. I could tell by the way she was looking at me. I looked for a way out. I will never forget how she toyed with me, saying, "Well, nobody's here except you and me." I tried to tell her, "But God can see this." Ignoring me, she unbuttoned the top skirt she was wearing, threw it over one of the idols, and draped it around his eyes, saying, "Now, the gods can't see any more."

How could I do this? How could I do this to the man who fed me? How could I dishonor him who cared for me and treated me like a son, even with my being a foreigner and an alien in his house? More importantly, how could I do this to my God? I laid God on her that day and, for a moment, she let me go. But unrelentingly, she kept on and on. This time, however, I put myself in a bad position, because there she was on the leopard skin chaise lounge, and when she called me, I came in by the door near the veranda where she was. She reached up, grabbed me by my cloak, and pulled me toward her. Although I'm bigger and stronger, that lady had strength from somewhere else. She pulled me down saying, "Have sex with me. I want you right now!" I started squirming. I pulled up and got away fast. The last thing I remember is that my cloak fell down as I ran out the door. I got out of there as fast as I could.

The strangest thing I heard ten yards off the property was her screaming like a panther, as if someone had his hands around her neck choking her to death. I didn't know whether to turn around or to keep running. Had some assailant come in to kill her? I did not know. I only knew that, within a matter of minutes, I saw an angry Potiphar, more angry than I had ever seen him before. Remember, Potiphar is the chief bodyguard; killing people is no problem for him. When I was seized, it brought back a rush of emotions. I remembered how my brothers grabbed me, bound and gagged me, and threw me into a pit. Now I am bound and gagged again, and thrown into prison. I demanded to know, "What's my crime? What's the charge?" "You attacked Potiphar's wife." "What? She's lying!" But when we returned to the house, her clothes were ripped, a bruise was visible on her shoulder, her mascara was running, and her lipstick was smeared. I cried, "I didn't do that." "She had your cloak," was the reply.

Oh, woe is me! I'm so tired of coats and cloaks! I was put in a pit because of a coat, now I'm in prison because of a cloak. I declare, I won't wear them anymore. This is the last time that I will ever get involved with coats and cloaks. I'm so glad my mother was a Langston Hughes fan. I can still hear her telling me, "Son, you'd best remember that life ain't no crystal stair." Life for me right now is no crystal stair. I am locked down for something

I didn't do, but I've learned a lot of lessons here. African American brothers, perhaps the greatest lesson I've learned that I want to leave with you, as I rehash some of my story, is simply this: I got to prison, even to Egypt, asking, "Where is God when you need him?" Prison not only motivates you to retrace the intricate details of your past; it also forges your faith.

I don't ask that question any more because I know the answer to it, and that is this: wherever I am, God is. I know this now. It doesn't matter where I am in life, God is there. I finally know what my father meant when he called God El, El Bethel. I now know what he meant when he called him El, the every awareness of God, El Shaddai, El Elyon, Elohim. I know that he was talking about an Almighty God who neither prison cells nor jail cells nor hospital rooms, pits nor problems, deserts nor wastelands nor wilderness can keep out. For wherever you are, God is. I learned that much about God.

No more do I ask the question, "Where is God?" Now I ask a more practical question, which is simply this: "Where am I when God needs me?" Where am I when God needs a witness in the world, a preacher in prison, a witness in jail, a celebration in the hospital room, or a testimony under bad conditions? Where am I when God needs somebody?

You learn a lot when you're on these long prison stays, my brothers. I'll share with you a couple of things that I have learned. I consider how my father and mother were, and I remember how fondly my father talked about my mother. I always wanted my own woman, my own wife, and my own family. But right now, it appears that this may never happen. I'm in chapter thirty-nine of my life. I don't know what's in store for me for chapters forty and forty-one. But in hindsight, I see that, even though I'm in a single position and living with it, I don't consider it a curse. I sometimes hear people talking about the curse of singleness. Not so. I get so tired of hearing this from young men who are only twenty-five, twenty-six, or twenty-seven. They constantly want to know, "When are you going to get married?" Many men believe that a mate will make them whole and complete. They remind you that you're getting older. "You should have some children; your biological clock is ticking down." But, I am different; I don't see my singleness as a permanent marital status. I look at singleness as a position that I'm in at the present moment. I don't know what my future holds, but I know this: I won't do anything just to make other people happy with who I am.

You hear those stories when you're locked up in prison. I'll just take anybody. They had best watch what they're saying; they might run into Potiphar's wife! They'd want no part of that, I guarantee. I learned some lessons in singleness that applies to anybody. I've learned it and I've applied it to my life, and it works out. It landed me in lockup, but if I had to do it all over again, I'd do the same thing.

This is what I learned about living single: I learned, first, to live relationally. I hear a lot of stories here in prison locked up, especially from people talking about relationships they've had. They've lived in relationships, but I'm talking about living relationally. Some of these fellows are here because they were dating a girl who simply spoke to some other man. They are in here because they killed the woman just because she spoke to somebody. I tell them, she's not a piece of property, and you don't own her. I tell them to live relationally and to do so in the sense that you meet people along your way. You don't know who you're meeting; they may be Pharaoh now, they may be a wicked brother now, but you don't know. God may be allowing you to meet all these different people because he has a purpose and a plan in which he wants to take you from down in the pit all the way up to the pinnacle. You don't know how he's going to use these people in your life in the future, so you, brothers, should be careful.

It is foolish to deal with a woman with fatal attractions who is so jealous and envious that, if she sees you shaking hands with somebody, she reacts violently. Live relationally. Live in a way that, if you come to the church with a friend, and you speak to a sister in the pew, by the time you get to the parking lot in the car, you don't have to answer numerous questions about who she is, where you met her, how you know her, and why she hugged you. Tell those questioning you, "If you went to church, you would know." Live relationally.

But, then, I learned by living single to live reliably. I have no regrets doing what I did in Potiphar's house. I ran out the door, and I'll run out the door again, even if it means being ostracized, laughed at, and having the finger pointed at me. I want to live reliably because my reliability does not rest on Mr. Potiphar's opinions of me alone. I have a higher order whom I must answer to. I could have gone ahead and had the woman, and nobody would have known about it, with the exception of two persons—God and myself!

As I've tried to tell other men, I knew that another man's wife was off limits from the start. Some men talked about what they would have done, but they don't have the kind of relationship with a holy God like I have. I don't derive my pleasure from the number of people I sleep with; it has nothing to do with that. My sense of worth is not dependent on how many folk I can conquer; it is based on how reliably God can trust me in the crunch of life. Can God depend on me? Each time I tell that part of the story, I don't usually get much help with it, because we live in a sex-crazed world. Here in prison, we have HBO; we can see "Sex In The City" where young women are with everybody they can be with, one night with him, and the next night with him, and the next night with him, and back and forth. That is today's standard modus operandi; but I want to live with God so that I can pre-serve my life with an element of purity. Whenever I come out of singleness, I don't want to have to find twenty folks who know my business and ask them not to divulge what we've been doing. I don't want to be ashamed of my singleness.

I learned one last thing, and that is how to live responsibly. More than my reliability and my relational living, my responsible lifestyle is what landed me in here. Potiphar put me over his house, and I worked the house even when he wasn't looking. I didn't try to fudge the timesheet; I didn't tell him I spent $50 on gas running errands when I was really casually rolling all over town. I'm here because I was responsible. I managed his resources right. I handled his relationships right. I dealt with his accoutrements right. I did all of that; I was responsible.

I had more time in my singleness than most folk who worked in the armed guard who had been married and had children. Brothers, I had more time in my singleness than they had. Therefore, I could give more of myself. In fact, when I would give myself to work and service, I found that, in those quiet moments when I backed away from working, I could go into my private room where I could spend more time in communion with God. I found out during those times that I would not have been able to make it if it had not been for the Lord, who's on my side.

I don't expect the person who lives on the surface of life to appreciate my life. Prison for me at first looked like it was a shutdown, a lockout, but I'm discovering that God has a picture of me, and prison is a dark room where he brings the negative so that it can be developed. Once the negative is developed, he's going to hold me up as a beautiful portrait for the world to see. I know that now, my brothers.

I wish I could spend more time talking to you, but I have to close this chapter. Let me tell you one last thing that I learned while in this cell. I don't know what chapter forty will bring in my life. I don't know what chapter forty-one is going to look like or chapter forty-two; all I can deal with today is chapter thirty-nine. Yet, I tell you what I learned while in this place. Right here, I learned that God gave me favor, even with the prison warden. You know what? Here I am now, the right hand of the warden. I have keys to walk in and out of the jail when I get ready. I can come and go, and I can eat with the butlers and bakers when I want to. I can taste the choicest meals because God has found favor with me.

I want to leave something with everybody, but especially with men who are in singleness today: Go and live single. Live relationally, live reliably, and live responsibly, wherever you are, whatever your position, condition, or place in life. If I could have talked to my brothers when I first got here, I probably would have uttered multiple expletives at them, but not anymore because, since I've been here, I've discovered that it was God who has been at work behind the scenes in my life. When I see Judah or Reuben or Dan or Gad or Simeon or Issachar again, I will tell them this, for I know they're going to be scared. I must tell them one thing, that when they did it to me in chapter thirty-eight of my life, they meant it for evil, but now that I'm going to get past chapter thirty-nine, the Lord told me to tell them that he meant it for good. "We know that all things work together for good for those who love God, who and are called according to his purpose" (Romans 8:28). Hallelujah!

Our decisions have a way of putting us in places and situations that were never part of our agenda, but the text is tailored to teach us that God is the sovereign one who is in control, and that he can turn all of our negatives into positives. Brothers, please know that wherever you are, you can live relationally, reliably, and responsibly before God. You may very well be single, but you are not alone. The Bible teaches us that God will never leave you nor forsake you. God also teaches us that wherever the spirit of the Lord is, there is liberty. You may be behind bars, but you're not alone. You may be single, but with God as your friend, you are not alone. You may be an older gentleman, but with God the Savior, you are not alone. Your parents may not be there for you, but with God as your rock, you are not alone.

Black men, look within yourself, see yourself as being relational, reliable, and responsible. After all, Jesus was relational when he introduced himself to you and your circumstances. After all, Jesus was reliable when he came down forty and two generations to save us from our sins. After all, Jesus was responsible when he stayed up on a rugged cross one Friday night and stayed in a borrowed tomb on Saturday but got up early Sunday morning with all power in his hands. With Jesus on your side, you can be single, but not alone! Amen!

chapter ten

getting to the RIGHT place
at the right time

jeremiah a. wright jr.

Then Samson called to the LORD and said, "Lord GOD, remember me and strengthen me only this once, O God, so that with this one act of revenge I may pay back the Philistines for my two eyes." And Samson grasped the two middle pillars on which the house rested, and he leaned his weight against them, his right hand on the one and his left hand on the other. Then Samson said, "Let me die with the Philistines." He strained with all his might; and the house fell on the lords and all the people who were in it. So those he killed at his death were more than those he had killed during his life. Then his brothers and all his family came down and took him and brought him up and buried him between Zorah and Eshtaol in the tomb of his father Manoah. He had judged Israel twenty years. (Judges 16:28–31, NRSV)

❦❦

samson was a man who a whole lot of men can relate to. Let's look at him for just a moment. Judges 15:20 says the same thing that Judges 16:31 says: Samson judged Israel for twenty years. In this period of Israel's history, there was no monarchy. There was no king, there was no capital, and there was no centralized form of government like there were in the days of King Saul, King David, and King Solomon.

In Samson's day, there were twelve loosely knit tribes, each one of them named after one of the sons or grandsons of Jacob. They had a loose federation, which biblical scholars call an "amphicty-onic relationship." That means that they would band together to fight as allies when it was absolutely necessary, but most of the time, if there was any fighting going on, it was the fighting that they did among themselves. The tribe of Dan would fight the tribe of Ephraim for a little while. That is the Bloods and the Crypts. The tribe of Reuben would fight the tribe of Benjamin for another little while. That is the Gangster Disciples and the Twelfth Street Gang.

In fact, if you look at the last verse in the Book of Judges, you will see the final exclamation point of a theme that is repeated over and over and over again. Judges 17:6, 18:1, 19:1, and 21:25 say the same thing. The writer says it over and over again. He says, "In those days there was no king in Israel; all the people did what was right in their own eyes." It was virtually an anarchy, and the only form of government that could stop the tribes from fighting each other or rally them together to fight a common ene-my was the person who sat in the office of judge. Some of Israel's greatest heroes and "sheroes" come from this time period, which is called the period of the judges.

Deborah, a preacher woman in chapter 4 of this great book, was one of the judges. Deborah led 10,000 men from the tribe of Naphtali and the tribe of Zebulun against Sisera, the general of Jabin's army. They kicked butt, and they took names.

Gideon, the son of Joash, was one of Israel's judges. Gideon took 32,000 men against the Midianites, and God told him, "You've got too many. Weed out the weak-hearted," and 22,000 men went home. God looked at the ten thousand who stayed with Gideon and said, "You've still got too many. Let's sift through them and see how many men are really ready to fight." Then 9,700 were sifted out and, with three hundred men, Gideon wiped out 120,000 of the enemy.

Samson ruled over this wild bunch of "do-whatever-you-feel-like-doing" folk for twenty years. He was successful in his professional life. For twenty years, no king, no authority, no binding covenants; it was a loose confederation that spent most of its time fighting each other. And for twenty years Samson judged Israel. He was successful in his professional life. Settling disputes, hearing cases, dispensing wisdom, and fighting when he had to, the brother could humbug now. Brother Samson could throw down when he wanted to and if he had to. In Judges 15, Samson took the jawbone of a donkey and killed 1,000 of the enemies all by himself. You talk about Rambo! You talk about Sylvester Stallone calling himself your worst nightmare! With no explosives and no modern firepower, with his bare hands and a donkey's jawbone, Samson put 1,000 of the enemies six feet under. The brother was bad!

He was a judge who was known all over. He was successful in his professional life, but he was a failure in his personal life. Samson was a man who a whole lot of us men can relate to. How many men do you know who have it all together as a professional? They seem to have been in the right place at the right time, and their profession has taken off like a rocket. Maybe it is because they went to the right schools and made all the right friends. Maybe it is because they knew how to network properly and they made all the right connections. Maybe it is because they were just plain old lucky and just happened to be in the right spot when the door of opportunity opened up. For whatever reason, they are doing great in their respective professions. Their income is in the six figures. They live in a fabulous house and they've got a fine wife. They've got 2.5 kids and a sports utility vehicle. They play golf with the corporate executive giants and they vacation on tropical islands or cruise ships or take ski trips. They belong to the Snow Gophers. They attend the ski summit. They wear $2,000 suits on their backs and $1,000 skins on their feet.

They are a success when it comes to their professional life, but they are failures when it comes to their personal lives. They've got it all together on the professional level, but on the personal level, their life is down the toilet. Samson was a man a whole lot of us men can relate to. Some of us try to cover up the shambles of our personal lives by drinking it away, by smoking it away, by sniffing it away or screwing it away, but nothing we do can take away the awful truth that we still have to live with every day—and that is that, on the personal level, our lives are down the toilet.

Samson had a "zipper problem." He thought below his waist rather than above his waist. I told you that Samson was a man that a whole lot of us can relate to. Walk with me from chapter 14 through 16. Look at how this brother's sex life ultimately messed up his whole life.

Chapter 14:1 says that Samson went down to Timnah, and at Timnah he saw a Philistine woman. Samson wanted to hook up with a woman who was his natural-born enemy! Put your finger here and go back one chapter to chapter 13. The angel of the Lord told Samson's mother, "[Your son] shall begin to deliver Israel from the hand of the Philistines" (Judges 13:5). The Philistines were the enemy. Chapter 14:4 says, "At that time the Philistines had dominion over Israel." The Philistines were the enemy. In Judges 14:19, Samson, with the Spirit of the Lord upon him, went down to Ashkelon. Ashkelon was one of the five main Philistine cities, and there in Ashkelon, Samson killed thirty men of that town. The Philistines were the enemy. Chapter 15:8 says, "[Samson] struck them down hip and thigh with great slaughter." The Philistines were the enemy. We just saw Judges 15:15 where Samson killed 1,000 Philistines all by himself. The Philistines were the enemy. But here in chapter 14:1, Samson has no conscience; he is thinking from below the waist.

Dr. Renita Weems-Espinosa says that, unfortunately, "When God created man, he gave him a brain and a penis, but he only gave enough blood so that one of those organs can function at a time." If the blood supply is rushing to one of those organs, then trust me, the other one ain't functioning. Samson saw a fine Philistine "tenderroni" and it was on.

Samson came home and told his parents, "I want you to go get a Philistine woman down in Timnah. Get her for me as my wife." Momma and Daddy were trying to reason with him, but his brain wasn't functioning. Look what they say: "Is there not a woman among your old kind? Boy, what's wrong with you!" Samson said to his father, "The LORD is my shepherd and I see what I want. She pleases me." In other words, "If it's good *to* you, then it's got to be good *for* you."

Samson was a man that a whole lot of us men can relate to. He listened to the lower part of his body and not the upper, so he started sleeping with the enemy. He married her. Now, how are you going to deliver God's people from the enemy when you are sleeping with the enemy? Samson, I am telling you, had a zipper problem.

In chapter 14, Samson got mad, and he went back home. Maybe that is a topic for another sermon, but Samson got angry at his wife. She nagged him as some wives will do. She nagged him and nagged him and nagged him, until he told her the secret to his riddle. And then she ran straight to her people and told her people. Her people were Philistines. Her husband was an Israelite from the tribe of Dan; her people were the enemy. Samson was sleeping with the enemy, and she ran straight and told her people. Where was her allegiance? With her people. Then Samson found out that she had told. Chapter 14 says, "In hot anger he went back to his father's house. And Samson's wife was given to his companion, who had been his best man" (Judges 14:19–20). In Judges 15:4, Samson caught three hundred foxes, took some torches, tied the foxes tail-to-tail, tied a torch in between each tail, set fire to the torches, and turned the foxes loose. With that heat burning up their behinds, the foxes took off and burned up the Philistines' grain, corn, wheat, vineyards, and olive groves. When the Philistines found out Samson had done that, they burned his wife and her father. His wife was dead, and that is when he "went postal" and killed 1,000 of them.

With Samson's wife dead, we take his zipper problem up a notch. Samson went to Gaza where he saw a prostitute, and he bought him some personal time with her. Samson had a zipper problem, I am telling you. But look again, not only was he buying some sex, but she was probably also a Philistine woman. Gaza was a Philistine city. Those Philistine woman must have been some kind of fine! I mean, drop dead gorgeous. But they were still the enemy. Samson had a zipper problem.

Then Samson fell in love with a woman in the Valley of Sorek whose name was Delilah. Samson had a zipper problem. Do you believe me yet? He was a success in his professional life, but he was a failure in his personal life. Both Philistines and Israelites lived in the Valley of Sorek, so we do not know if for certain Delilah was a Philistine or not, but there are two things the text does tell us that we can see very easily.

First, the word *Delilah* is related to an Arabic root that means "flirt." Samson fell in love with a flirt. First, he was in bed with a woman of ill repute; then he was in love with a flirt. I am in the Word! Secondly, we also know that Delilah went into business with the lords of the Philistines to betray him. Look at chapter 16:5. She went into business, so if she was not a Philistine, that makes it even worse: She was an Israelite who sold her man out to the enemy for a price. In the first part of chapter 16, Samson was in bed with a woman of ill repute and, from verse 4 on, he was hooked up with another kind of woman. Both of the women did what they did for money—and Samson kept coming back.

When it came to women, Samson majored in bad choices. He made one bad choice after another, after another. Samson had a zipper problem, and I am telling you that I know a whole lot of men can relate to this problem. Let's not try to be so holy that we miss the point. Too many of us been there and done that. In fact, some of us are still there and still doing it!

Now, Delilah was fine. I mean Delilah was what we used to call in the Marine Corps "hubcap fine." She was beautiful! Delilah was hubcap fine, but Samson behaved foolishly.

Delilah was fine, but Samson was a fool. Look how many times she tried to set him up. First, the seven fresh bowstrings trick (Judges 16:9). The lords of the Philistines brought Delilah seven fresh bowstrings, and she tied him up. Why would a man let a woman tie him up? Second was the new rope trick. She tied him again, and the fool kept coming back. Trick three was the weaving of the seven dreadlocks. He was a genius in his professional life, but an idiot in his personal life. Fine is fine, but don't be no fool over fine, or your life is going right down the toilet.

Look at Samson's problem now from a theological and hermeneutical perspective: He had misplaced priorities because of his fixation on his lower extremities. Do you know what Samson's priority was supposed to have been? Look back in Chapter 13:5 again. The angel of God, the messenger of God, brings a word from God that Samson should be a Nazirite dedicated to God from birth. A Nazirite is one who is separated, set apart, in dedication to God. A Nazirite is one who is consecrated to serve God. A Nazirite is one for whom God comes first. God is priority.

Lest you start feeling off the hook because you ain't a Nazirite, let me remind you of two things Jesus said that also pertained to African American men and their priorities. God comes first. The two greatest commandments, Jesus said, are, first, "Thou shalt love the Lord thy God with all thy heart, with all thy soul, and with all thy mind." Second, "Love thy neighbor as thou loveth thyself" (see Mark 12:28–31).

Jesus also taught us to "seek first the kingdom of God and his righteousness, and all these things [when you put God first] will be added unto you" (see Matthew 6:33). God should be every man's number one priority. That is what Jesus said. Listen to what God says in Malachi 3:10: "Bring the full tithe into the storehouse, so that there may be food in my house, and thus put me to the test, says the LORD of hosts; see if I will not open the windows of heaven for you and pour down for you an over-flowing blessing." But some of us, like Samson, have misplaced priorities because our fixation is on our personal priorities. We are so busy trying to get over, to get some, to get a piece that we push God way down on the priority list. Samson had misplaced priorities because of his fixation on his private parts.

Samson lost sight of his purpose because he was too busy watching "poohnanny." He felt that the sisters had to "back that thing up!" What was his purpose? We have already seen it. God said it was that he, Samson, would begin to deliver Israel from the hands of the Philistines. That was his purpose. That's why God sent him. That's why he was born. He was born to be a deliverer, but he kept trying to be a lover. He lost sight of his pur-pose by keeping his eye on the "poohnanny."

Brothers, don't act "holier than thou." Some of us live right here on Samson's street. We lose sight of our purpose as men. We lose sight of our purpose as warriors. We lose sight of our pur-pose as providers. We lose sight of our purpose as fathers. We lose sight of our purpose as husbands. We lose sight of our purpose as Christians. We can't even worship sometimes because we got our eye on a sister over there; we desire to exchange telephone numbers right after the benediction.

Samson forgot his destiny because he was focused in on his "manhood." Samson forgot about fulfilling his destiny because his focus was on satisfying his selfish, misplaced desires. Look at Judges 13:24. The Lord blessed Samson. This was his destiny, given miraculously by God. The angel said, "Although you are barren, having born no children, you shall conceive and bear a son" (Judges 13:3). You talk about planned parenthood! God planned this pregnancy. Samson was given miraculously by God. This was his destiny: born to be set aside as one sanctified for God's plan. This was his destiny—born to be consecrated from birth as a man with God's mark upon his life. This was his destiny.—born to be a deliverer in the holy history of Israel. This was his destiny. The Lord blessed him. This was his destiny. The Spirit of the Lord came upon him to give him supernatural strength. This was his destiny. But Samson forgot his destiny because his focus was on his fleshly desires.

Brothers, you may have the Samson Street blues right now, because your focus has not been where it should have been. But that is not all that there is to this story. You see, God had to get Samson in the right place before Samson could do the right thing. Sometimes God has to bring us down to a place where we are forced to face the fact that we need God. As men, we need God. As African American men, we need God. As the number one enemy of the state in this country, we need God. In order to make it from one day to the next, we need God. But how can God help us and use us unless we are in the right place at the right time?

As husbands, we need God. As lovers, we need God. As workers, we need God. As warriors, we need God. As providers, we need God. As fathers, we need God. As sons, we need God. As brothers, we need God. As believers, we need God!

Sometimes, like Samson, God has to get us to the right place before we are able to recognize our greatest need in this life. Our greatest need is not for more money. Our greatest need is not for a bigger house. Our greatest need is not for an understanding mate. Our greatest need is for God, and we are at the right place when we recognize that.

That is where Samson was in Judges 16:28. He was at the right place. He was at a place where he acknowledged that he needed God. Not good loving, but God. Not good looks, but God. Not all the right curves at just the right angles, but God. Not a groove, but God. And when he recognized that need, he called on the Lord. And that is what I call the right time.

The right time is when you call on the Lord—wherever you call on the Lord. Like the prodigal son in Luke 15, Samson was in a pigpen. That was the right place, and he came to himself. He realized that he had a father who would provide, so he arose at the right time and went back to the right place. Elijah, on Mt. Horeb, running from Queen Jezebel, was in the right place, and he called on the Lord at the right time. Three Hebrew boys were in a fiery furnace. That's the right place, and they called on the Lord at the right time.

The right place is anywhere that you are. The right time is whenever you call on him. Why? Because whenever you call and wherever you are when you call, you don't have to worry about it; God is already there. You can call him right now; he's already here.

Let me tell you something. While you were out purchasing or borrowing this book, God was with you. He was waiting on you to get here all at the same time. He was already there. Whatever you need, you ask him; he's already there. He answered Samson, and he will answer you. He answered Shadrach, Meshach, and Abednego, and he will answer you. He answered Elijah, and he will answer you. My African American brothers, no time is better than now to get to the right place. My brothers, no place is better than where you are to call on Jesus at the right time.

chapter eleven

the bigness of GOD

donald j. washington

> After leaving the synagogue he entered Simon's house. Now Simon's mother-in-law was suffering from a high fever, and they asked him about her. Then he stood over her and rebuked the fever, and it left her. Immediately she got up and began to serve them. As the sun was setting, all those who had any who were sick with various kinds of diseases brought them to him; and he laid his hands on each of them and cured them. (Luke 4:38–40, NRSV)

∞

it is without question that we live in a society where the majority of the people desire a quick fix to their problems, trials, and tribulations. It appears as though people would much rather read a multitude of "How-to" books, call psychics, visit palm readers and fortune tellers, and watch self-help, 30-minute TV shows with ill-advised hosts rather than read the Bible, attend church, and seek the spiritual advice of a pastor. It is clear, my brothers, that many people, including black men, are looking for God in all the wrong places!

Many parents would rather cast their lots on how to rear their children upon the secular lips of talk show hosts as opposed to the directives that we find in the trusted pages of our holy writ that we know as the Bible. And sadly, when we as a collective body of believers turn to the Bible, we seem to choose and meditate on those portions of the Bible that allow us to make use of the most expedient, popular, and least demanding resolutions that can be digested within a Christian context. We, as a nation and as a people, seem to look for the answers that plague our country, state, city, neighborhood, church, school, home, and family through every and any medium that comes into our lives that has a Christian connotation attached to it or upon it, regardless of its credibility. In other words, we have allowed ourselves to fall for any "hooks and sinkers" imaginable. To avoid availing ourselves to the word of God, we would rather spend thousands of dollars to hear a motivational speaker or a powerless-for-profit prophet. Likewise, we are more inclined to read an autobiography of a popular celebrity than meditate on the book of Psalms, Proverbs, or Job. The prevailing consensus, the earthly agreement, is that a psychologist, psychiatrist, pharmacist, philosopher, biologist, or even a musician can help us to come to a better understanding of our dilemmas than the Bible itself, or a preacher of the Bible.

But I must remind you that the Bible is still the number one best-selling book in the world, as it should be! The content of this book is still a reliable source for addressing the chiliad of ills that test our faith on a daily basis. The Bible is still the most reliable source for learning and teaching the appropriate conduct to display at all times. The answer to what is tearing away at your joy can still be found in the man we call Jesus the Christ, the Holy One, the Bearer of Good News, the One who was there in the beginning and the One who will be there in the end, the Alpha and the Omega. God has proven to be bigger than all that we can possibly imagine! The question becomes, How big is your God?

The text suggests at least three possibilities of how God can manifest himself to a troubled saint. One, God is big enough to meet you in a public form and forum. Two, God is big enough to meet you in your house, in a private form and forum. Three, God is big enough to meet you in the privacy of you, in a personal form and forum.

Your miracle could come from anywhere and at anytime. Black men, although you may have doubts, your human situation is no match for God's unchanging hand. God can meet you anywhere at anytime, and he can deliver you from anything and anybody. God will love you, regardless of who you are, and God will continue to be by your side anyhow, anyway, and at any place. You, my brothers, must believe that Jesus' authority can transcend through and over any man-made powers or barriers.

God is big enough to meet you in a public form or forum. He can pick you out of a crowd and bless you right then and there. He is, without question, a mighty God! The first place that Jesus displays his authority is in the synagogue. There is a man possessed with a demon inside the synagogue, what is equivalent in the text to the church today. Jesus shows us that his authority extends over the powers of those who represent evil, even in the church. For the demons recognized who he was and obeyed him.

My brothers in Christ, you must know and believe that wherever there is Jesus, there is liberty. He has paid a price for you and for me. Your very beings, my brothers, belong to him. God is big enough to bless you at anytime during the worship experience. A guest in church can experience God when an usher hands him or her the program. God can manifest himself during the welcoming of our guests. It may be in a song when individuals feel the touch of God upon their hearts. But God is not limited to the arena of the church. The civic center, the science museum, the courthouse, and the fitness center could get a visit from God on any day.

Your breakthrough and blessing could come just when you are about to use your credit card to buy a suit that you are only buying to impress a young lady. God will drop his spirit upon you and remind you that you are committing a sin called material gluttony. That is when you will remember that little boy or little girl who needs a pair of shoes or a jacket. Humans call that shift in perspective a conviction, but God calls it a blessing because you shift your will to his will. And his will is that we should all bear one another's burdens and look to be a blessing to those who are less fortunate than ourselves. I don't know about you, but the last time that I checked, the earth is the Lord's and the fullness thereof, and it all belongs to him. We are all conduits for how God desires to use us.

God could show up in the streets of your city because he said "greater is he that is in you, than he that is in the world." God can go anywhere that you take him. He can go into our hospitals, jails, shelters, and even on the basketball courts. Jesus needs our testimonies out there, in the streets, in the trenches, in the institutions! He understood something that all black men need to understand today: God saves people so that people can assist him with their testimonies in order that others may be saved as well.

Not only is God big enough to deal with the public arena of our lives, he is also big enough to meet you in your house, in private. The text says that after leaving the synagogue, Jesus went to Simon's mother-in-law's house, and she was stricken with a fever. The text says that he stood over her and, with just a word, he rebuked the fever; and it left her immediately, and she began to minister unto him. There are two salient points to this portion of the pericope. First, when God delivers you, he expects something in return. Second, your house is not off-limits to the presence of God. This is why the psalmist writes in Psalm 139: 7–12:

Where can I go from your spirit? Or where can I flee from your presence? If I ascend to heaven, you are there; if I make my bed in Sheol, you are there. If I take the wings of the morning and settle at the farthest limits of the sea, even there your hand shall lead me, and your right hand shall hold me fast. If I say, "Surely the darkness shall cover me, and the light around me become night," even the darkness is not dark to you; the night is as bright as the day, for darkness is as light to you.

God will show up at your house without an invitation. He'll sit at your table and dine with you, but the question is, will you recognize him? Will you welcome him? And if so, will you serve him?

God is so big! This is why we say that he is omnipresent and omnipotent. He has all powers; he knows all things. There is no rock that you can hide under because God is the rock of your salvation. There is no door that you can close to escape him, for he is a door when every other door has been closed. His love is the key that opens all doors. The Bible says that faith, charity, and love are all great, but the greatest of them is love. Brothers, love knows no bounds, and "God so loved the world, that he gave his only begotten Son, that whosoever believeth in him should not perish, but have everlasting life" (John 3:16, KJV).

God is big enough to move the land that your house sits on. That is why Joshua said, "As for me and my household, we will serve the LORD" (Joshua 24:15). It is in your house where you can receive his blessing or his wrath. Your house is not off-limits to God. That is why my grandmother always said, "Don't throw stones at glass houses" and "You better get your own house in order because you don't know when he's coming back."

God is not only big enough to bless you in a public form and in a private form; he can also bless you in a personal form. Look at the text—the disciples brought many people to Jesus. The text says that Jesus touched them personally. Many black men feel that our problems or situations are too unique for God. We feel that he really can't help us with our problems. But God is big enough to become small enough to handle and to deliver us from our self-defined and unique situation. Let us not forget what God told Moses when Moses asked the question to God, "Who shall I say sent me?" God said, "Tell the Hebrews, the black people, that the God of Abraham, Isaac, and Jacob, has sent you."

Then God goes on to say to Moses, "I am that I am," which simply means that "I will be what you need me to be, when you need me to be it." I am your alarm clock in the morning. I am the author and finisher of your faith. I am the fulfillment that comforts you after you eat and drink. I am your peace that surpasses all understanding. I am your friend when you feel that you have no friends. I am the truth, the light, and the way. I am Yahweh—your God of the mountains. I am your Jehovah-Jireh, your provider, the God of your valleys. I am your dreams for a better tomorrow. I am your good shepherd who watches over you, day and night. I am your joy in the midst of your pain. I am the ruler and controller of your destiny. I am the one who loves you like no one else can. I am your healer and deliverer. I am your sanity in the midst of chaos, for I am not a God of confusion. I am your water when you are thirsty. I am your bread when you are hungry. I am truth in the midst of lies. I am the father of all luminaries—the moon, stars, and the sun. I am the light when there is darkness all around you. I am life in the presence of death. I am your precious Lord. I am that I am.

chapter twelve

cast THY bread upon the waters

otis moss jr.

Send out your bread upon the waters, for after many days you will get it back. (Ecclesiastes 11:1, NRSV)

✪✪

the difference between greatness and mediocrity is learning to serve. The difference between selfishness and unselfishness is learning to give. To serve is to be great, my brothers. To give is to grow in grace. It is possible in a materialistic culture to confuse bribery with true giving. Giving makes us rich, not always in stocks and bonds, but always in strength, purpose, and fulfillment.

The text in Ecclesiastes 11:1 has been repeated millions of times across the ages. And there are three perspectives on this text that I would like to lift up briefly and then underscore. I want to examine the three ways that we, African American men, should learn to give. When I gave this message at Olivet Institutional Baptist Church, where I have been privileged to serve for twenty-seven years, I presented it in parts one and two. However, believing that the seeing eye can possibly embrace more in ten to twelve minutes than the listening ear can tolerate or endure in twenty to thirty minutes, I will risk sharing three perspectives and three points.

One perspective on "cast your bread upon the waters" is the wisdom of sowing and reaping, planting and harvesting. Cast your seeds of service across the field of life. Do not wait until you have mastered the mysteries of nature before you plant. Do not postpone the blessings of planting until you know all there is to be known about earth, wind, sun, soil, seasons, day, and night. This is a multi-million-year discovery process, and we, my brethren, come into this world for a fleeting moment. Therefore, we must plant with the urgency of now.

This notion about our fleeting lives was true in the first century when Paul wrote to the Christians in Corinth, and it is true in the twenty-first century. "We know in part and we understand in part," although knowledge, wisdom, and reason should precede momentous decisions, strategic plans, and serious commitments. In other words, we cannot wait until we know all there is to be known about life before starting a family. Nor can we wait to know all there is to be known about God before preaching a sermon. Cast your bread upon the water now, even if you have just a half loaf, a slice, or a few crumbs! We must plant and labor and leave the consequences in the hands of God.

The second perspective is to launch our ships out upon the waters of incalculable possibilities. We cannot serve at our highest and best if we remain in sheltered shores and isolated home ports. My African American brothers, Jesus challenges us to "launch out into the deep" (see Luke 5:4). "Go into all the world" (Mark 16:15). "Ye shall be my witnesses unto…the uttermost part of the earth" (Acts 1:8, KJV). If we are to be global citizens with the courage to lead as black men, we must cast our bread upon the waters. With spiritual sensitivity and prophetic vision, cast your bread upon the waters. My brothers, I would rather launch my ship into the deep waters and go down in a storm than remain in the harbor and drowse to death.

The third perspective is that we must be generous as servants of God. Prosperity without generosity is robbery! Wealth without worthiness is shameful! Our Savior teaches us to whom much is given, much is required. Bread is not to be hoarded; it must be shared. Bread becomes bitter and stale if not shared. If we cast it upon the waters, it can return in the rivers, lakes, and seas in all forms of sea life, blessing multitudes and nations far beyond our time and space. Bread shared is holy. Bread shared in love is living bread incarnate that feeds the whole person. If we cast our bread upon the waters, we share in feeding all humankind. And when we, my brothers, cast our bread upon the waters for all humankind, we cast it at the feet of Jesus. "Send out your bread upon the waters."

There are three great and gracious ways of giving. Giving and service are holy and inseparable. First, there is internal giving, which is self-development. We need to give to ourselves as part of taking care of God's image—the temple of God in the time and space we occupy. The mind is precious and deserves to be filled with truth, and truth blesses us and makes us free. Truth is mighty! Truth is militant! Trust is majestic! But truth is more than these. Jesus said, "I am the way, and the truth, and the life" (John 14:6). What greater gift can we give to ourselves than to bring ourselves into the presence of Christ? If we fill our minds with truth, our hearts with hope, and our lives with love, we can truly cry out, "My soul is a witness for my Lord!" Give internally with wholesome self-esteem and healthy self-development.

The second way of giving is externally. Give to each other. We are one body, many members. We are one spirit, many gifts. We need each other. Isolation and alienation are in conflict with the will of God and the spirit of Jesus Christ. One of our beloved members of Olivet gladly states, "I am blessed to be a blessing." We are given to give. Internal giving is receiving. External giving is sharing. Every great institution is the product of external giving.

Elizabeth Evelyn Wright cast her bread upon the waters of Denmark, South Carolina, and Vorhees College was born. Mary McLeod Bethune cast her bread upon the waters of Daytona Beach, Florida, and Bethune Cookman College was born. Laurence C. Jones, "the little professor," cast his bread upon the waters of the state of Mississippi, surrounded by the Ku Klux

Klan, and Piney Woods Country Life School was born. African American men, cast your bread upon the waters in your time and in your space.

There is a third form of giving that I choose to call eternal giving. Eternal giving is to take all that we are, and all that we have, and all that we hope to be, and to use it to the glory of God. Eternal giving is to take our internal gifts and being, as well as our external gifts, and to use them according to the Scripture which says, "Honor the Lord with thy substance and with the firstfruits of all thine increase" (Proverbs 3:9). Eternal giving says, "Take my life and let it be consecrated Lord to thee." Eternal giving says with Paul, "For me to live is Christ and to die is gain" (Philippians 1:21). Eternal giving declares, "My witness is in heaven and my record is on high." It is in Christ that our gifts will last. Only what we do in Christ and through Christ will last.

When we give internally, externally, and eternally, we "cast our bread upon the waters." We do so eternally by dedicating our lives to truth, love, justice, and reconciliation.

chapter thirteen

thank god for BOAZ, a real man of god

timothy j. clarke

Now Naomi had a kinsman on her husband's side, a prominent rich man, of the family of Elimelech, whose name was Boaz. (Ruth 2:1, NRSV)

∞

whenever i read ruth 2:1, the thought comes to me, "Thank God for Boaz." Why? Because, to me, Boaz represents a prototype of what I believe every man—every black man—should be striving for.

There are a lot of people who believe that the black family is on its way down (or is already down) and that there is no hope. But I am not ready to preach the funeral for the black family. There are many people who believe that black men are on their way out and they have no future. Again, I am not ready to preach the funeral for black men. I believe that God is at work reclaiming and transforming black men who are now finding out both who they are and whose they are. Black men are beginning to realize that when God made us, he did not make a mistake. We are special in the sight of God. God is no respecter of persons and there is nothing men cannot achieve with God's help, regardless of their skin color. We must stop using race as an excuse and begin to believe what the Bible says: "I can do all things through him who strengthens me" (Philippians 4:13).

I am convinced that most black men are not on drugs, in jail, beating their wives, or molesting their children. God still has some real men—men who realize that no matter what they were in the past, once they met Jesus, he changed their lives. I still believe that Jesus makes the difference! A drug addict before Christ now has victory. An alcoholic before Christ now has victory. The blood of Jesus Christ saves, delivers, and restores.

My brothers in Christ, it does not matter what else you have going for you—money, houses, cars—if you do not have Jesus Christ in your life, you have nothing! A man without Jesus is a failure! Sometimes we believe that if we possess material things, we will be successful. Often, we fail to remember that there is a difference between the success that the world gives versus the success that God gives. Whatever the world gives, it can take away. If the world elevates you, it can bring you down. If the world promotes you, it can demote you. If the world makes you great, it will last for only fifteen minutes. But when God blesses you, there is nothing the world can do about it!

I read a book by Samuel Friedman, *Upon This Rock,* which is the story of the St. Paul Community Baptist Church and of Johnny Ray Youngblood in Brooklyn, New York. Youngblood took a church in the ghetto—one of the worst in the city—and turned it around, drawing hundreds of black men who were former con artists, pimps, pushers, hustlers, and addicts into the church. Youngblood says that one of the reasons more black men don't come to church is because they haven't found anyone in the Bible or the pew with whom they can relate.

One of the worst things that happens to men when they get saved is that they stop acting like men. Sometimes when men get saved, they change their behavior. In the world, they were rough and tough, played baseball and basketball, and were as bad as they wanted to be. When these same men got saved, they became quiet and docile. In the world, we couldn't shut you up because you had an opinion about everything. Now you sit at church and never murmur a word. Listen, brothers, when a man gets saved,

Jesus does not make him less of a man; he makes him more of a man. Whatever you did well in the world, you ought to bring those same talents under subjection to Christ. If you played basketball in the world, you ought to "be like Mike" now that you are saved. We can't reach men because the men in the church act so unlike real men sometimes. You will never be able to help other men because you're not being real. The reason God saves us and leaves us in this world is so that we can reach back and help somebody else who is in the same shape we were in.

Johnny Ray Youngblood says that, in order to reach more men, we have to make the men in the Bible and the men in the pews relevant to the men in the world. These men want to identify with the Bible; they want a relationship with men in the Bible and the church. We need to be able to relate to men on their level. When I look at the life of Boaz, I see the kind of man I think all men should strive to be, and I'll tell you why: Boaz was a man of wealth, compassion, and integrity.

Boaz was a man of wealth. As a matter of fact, the Bible says that Boaz was a man of great wealth: "Now Naomi had a kinsman on her husband's side, a prominent rich man, of Elimelech, whose name was Boaz" (Ruth 2:1). Boaz was not a man on welfare or living from paycheck to paycheck; he was a man of means and substance. Sometimes men believe that in order to have a nice car, house, or clothes, they have to obtain it by unlawful means. Boaz was a man of wealth because he knew how to handle and manage money.

Men need to develop knowledge about money. Most men who are struggling financially do so because they don't know how to manage the money they have. We appear to be notorious for living beyond our means. We are forever living two paychecks ahead of homelessness. We walk around with $400 alligator shoes, designer suits, silk shirts, and gold around our neck, but if the stores wanted to, they could stop us in the middle of the street and strip us naked because we ain't paid a dime on none of it. To become a man of wealth, you must learn to handle what you have now, brothers. God will not bless you with more until you learn how to handle what you already have.

Boaz knew that all wealth is not necessarily material. The Hebrew word for wealth in Ruth 2 is *chayil,* which not only means "great material possessions," but also "a mighty man of valor, one strong in strength." In other words, Boaz was not just rich with money, he was rich in his reputation, his character, and his lifestyle. There are some "poor" rich men in this world because they have no scruples or morals. There are men with lots of money who are not wealthy. There are drug pushers who could buy and sell most people, but they are not wealthy. Wealth is more than what is in your pocket; it's what is in your heart. If you don't have a lot of money, don't go on a guilt trip, because money doesn't necessarily make you rich. You can be rich in the love of your family, in the respect of your friends, and in the approval of those who know you.

Then Boaz said to Ruth, "Now listen, my daughter, do not go to glean in another field or leave this one, but keep close to my young women. Keep your eyes on the field that is being reaped, and follow behind them. I have ordered the young men not to bother you. If you get thirsty, go to the vessels and drink from what the young men have drawn." ... At mealtime Boaz said to her, "Come here, and eat some of this bread, and dip your morsel in the sour wine." So she sat beside the reapers, and he heaped up for her some parched grain. She ate until she was satisfied, and she had some left over. When she got up to glean, Boaz instructed his young men, "Let her glean even among the standing sheaves, and do not reproach her. You must also pull out some handfuls for her from the bundles, and leave them for her to glean, and do not rebuke her." (Ruth 2:8–9,14–16)

Boaz met Ruth, sent her out into the fields, and instructed his servants to drop a few sheaves on purpose and for them not to let anybody else pick them up. That's compassion. Most men think compassion makes them weak and sets them up for someone to take advantage of them. After all, the stereotype goes that "real men are rough and tough and hard as steel. We never cry. We never express our feelings. Nothing bothers us." Personally, I don't want to be around any man who doesn't know how to cry, who is so hard that nothing breaks his heart. Being compassionate is not being a sissy. Jesus asked the question about the good Samaritan, "Who showed compassion?—the one who saw the man and did something about his condition" (see Luke 10:30–37).

You may be thinking, "I'm only one man. What can I do? I see the gangs, the violence, and the drugs. What can I do about it?" Brother, let me just suggest that one man can make a difference. One man can be a big brother. One man can coach little league. One man can tutor for a few hours every week. One man can teach Sunday school. One man can get children and youth together for an educational, recreational, or social outing. You do not need a preacher's license to do some good in the kingdom!

God has given men a certain power and authority. If you don't believe me, just think of how many times the mother asks her children to do something and usually has to repeat the request several times; but the father says it once and it's a done deal. Brother in Christ, even if you are divorced, do not stop helping to raise your children. Your absence demands your involvement more than at any other time. Recently, the newspaper in my city ran an article about the percentage of children in our school system that came from single-parent homes and, while the numbers were in and of themselves startling and astounding, what was even more disheartening was the performance level of these children. The report showed that these children scored lower on tests, performed at lower levels in class and on homework, and had more behavioral problems. Now would the presence of a father and a mother in their life solve all of these problems? Maybe not, but I just have to believe it would make a difference. The Bible talks about the "blessing," which were words spoken over the son by the father, and only he could bestow the blessing. How many of our sons and daughters have sought in so many places, in so many ways, for that blessing, the affirmation that comes only from a father? Brothers, if you have children, whether they live with you or not, take time with and for them. You have a place that no one else can fill!

Boaz was a man of compassion because he saw a need and met it. I wish more men would do that. There is so much going on in the world today, and all we need is for some men to see a need and be willing to do something about it.

Boaz was a man of integrity. He said to Ruth,

"All that you have done for your mother-in-law since the death of your husband has been fully told me, and how you left your father and mother and your native land and came to a people that you did not know before. May the LORD reward you for your deeds, and may you have a full reward from the LORD, the God of Israel, under whose wings you have come for refuge!" (Ruth 2:11–12).

The preceding two verses show us how Boaz related to Ruth. His actions were so different from many men today. Here was a man of wealth, position, and power. Ruth was a stranger and a foreigner, a poor widow. Boaz could have taken advantage of her. He could have asked, "You hungry? I've got food. You don't have a house? I've got a house. You need some clothes? Here's my credit card." He could have said, "Baby, as fine as you are, with that body you've got, listen honey, take my whole wallet! And when they give you two keys to your apartment, just give me one and, every now and then, I'll just stop by to check on you."

Boaz could have used his money to misuse Ruth, but he was a man of integrity. That's what I'm praying for—men who don't just have integrity at the church house, but at their house; men who don't just have integrity on Sunday, but Monday through Saturday, too; men who are not interested in pimping the women in the church by taking advantage of their vulnerability and playing with their emotions and affections to massage their own egos.

One of the reasons people don't take Christians seriously is because we talk out of both sides of our mouths. We are holier than thou on Sunday and lower than dirt on Monday. The world says, "I don't understand this. How can you sing Zion's songs on Sunday and cuss like a sailor on Monday? How can you lift holy hands on Sunday and then hold a cigarette or an alcoholic beverage or play the lottery with those same hands on Monday?" If we are going to make a difference in this world, then the world must see a difference. The way we live and carry ourselves must show that we have been changed by the power of God.

A real man has integrity. A real man learns how to treat women—your mother, your wife, your sister, your daughter, and the women in the church. Boaz was a man of integrity because he didn't try to play around with Ruth. Men have to do better by women. We have to stop painting women into corners, making empty promises, stringing three and four along at the same time. Instead, we have to develop some integrity.

I'll close by reminding you that Boaz was from Bethlehem, which is good news. If you read the entire book of Ruth, you'll see that Boaz is like another man from Bethlehem whose name is Jesus. God used Boaz to show us what Jesus was going to be like.

You know that Jesus is a man of wealth because he is the Son of God. He has angels that worship and adore him. The cattle on a thousand hills belong to him, and the hills on which they stand are his. Before there was a world, there was Jesus. And the Bible tells us that, "For you know the generous act of our Lord Jesus Christ, that though he was rich, yet for your sakes he became poor, so that by his poverty you might become rich" (2 Corinthians 8:9).

Jesus was a man of compassion because he looked beyond my faults and saw my needs. When I look at Boaz, I don't just see Boaz; I see another man from Bethlehem whose name is Jesus! The Lily of the Valley, the Bright and Morning Star, who gave his life that I might be saved. He hung on a cross that I might be redeemed. He gave his blood that I might be washed whiter than snow.

Now, I don't know how you feel about it, but I'm glad for Jesus. He saved me. He picked me up, turned me around, and placed my feet on solid ground. Because of Jesus, one day I'll stand before God and hear him say, "Well done, good and faithful servant."

And Jesus was a man of integrity. What is integrity? I suppose the word that I most like to use is *soundness;* it has to do with being whole, complete, without duplicity. When you look at the life of Jesus, that is what you see: a whole and balanced person. That's why Jesus is my hero, because he is a brother from the 'hood who had the capacity to be both whole and balanced. The New Testament talks about Jesus growing in stature and in favor with God. Do you see the balance in his life? Mentally, physically, spiritually, and relationally, Jesus had it going on. That is the model, the paradigm for African American men to follow—a balanced, whole brother, a man of integrity!

Boaz was a man of wealth, compassion, and integrity. That's the kind of man God is looking for today. Is that the kind of man you are right now? Is that the kind of man you want to be? That's the kind of man Boaz was. That's the kind of man Jesus was. That's the kind of man Booker T. Washington was; the kind of man Frederick Douglas was; the kind of man A. Philip Randolph, Marcus Garvey, Adam Powell, Roy Wilkins, Martin L. King, Malcolm and Medgar Evers were. All of these men were the kind of men we can honor, respect, and follow. They were men with issues, faults, and failings, but they were men who tried, loved, cared, shared, and gave. They were real men, saved men, godly men, and men like us, if we let God lead and use us. Thank God for Boaz!

chapter fourteen

the burden BEARER

darryl d. sims

Moses heard the people weeping throughout their families, all at the entrances of their tents. Then the LORD became very angry, and Moses was displeased. So Moses said to the LORD, "Why have you treated your servant so badly? Why have I not found favor in your sight, that you lay the burden of all this people on me? Did I conceive all this people? Did I give birth to them, that you should say to me, 'Carry them in your bosom, as a nurse carries a sucking child,' to the land that you promised on oath to their ancestors? Where am I to get meat to give to all this people? For they keep weeping to me and say, 'Give us meat to eat!' I am not able to carry all this people alone, for they are too heavy for me." (Numbers 11:10–14, NRSV)

❊❊

my beloved brothers, it is safe to say that we live in a time when many of us simply do not know where to turn for answers. The pressures of the world have produced some troubled people—people who are burdened and weighed down by anger, dissatisfaction, envy, jealousy, bigotry, selfishness, greed, guilt, and self-hatred. These people do not always like themselves. These people do not always like you and me. These people do not like too much authority in their lives. These people do not like a lot of discipline in their daily comings and goings. These people will smile in your face, while all the time trying to take your place. These people are backstabbers and backsliders. These people desire to be good, but they can't quite bring themselves to do what they know to be the right thing. These people are carrying around a lot of pain from yesterdays and yesteryears. These people know you by your first name and still will not speak to you as they pass by.

These people are given the awesome task of loving you when you don't want to be loved, when you don't deserve to be loved. These people are told to suffer in the name of someone else on a daily basis. Some of these people are around you all the time. These people are the ones who claim to surrender their very all to Jesus, but continue to complain about how they can't solve their own problems. These people are good people, but they can't always find good around them. These people possess a deep sense of obligation to assist the poor, but they find it difficult to fit the poor into their schedules. These people may very well be on their way to heaven, not because they deserve to go or have earned the right to go, but because somebody paid a heavy price for them to go to heaven, when Christ died on an old rugged cross.

Yes, my beloved brothers, "these people" to whom I have made reference are you and me; these people are our own brothers and sisters who are in the body of Christ. I stand here neither to judge you nor to condemn you. But if we are to be honest, we must admit that it is hard being a Christian, and it is hard to live in a sin-sick world.

Brothers, we all have some relatives in our lives who do some of the most awful things in the whole world. You look at the things that they are doing with their lives, to their lives, in their lives, and you say, "Help me, Lord Jesus, from taking somebody out of this world." And that's when you discover that you stand in need of a "burden bearer." Five hundred milligrams of Tylenol, Excedrin, Bayer Aspirin, or Motrin will not relieve the burden that is pounding away at your head and heart. Even the all-out "Pardon me, Lord, let me sip a little bit of this rum and coke

Smirnoff or Jack Daniels" (that you "have in your house for your friends") will not relieve the burden that rests and abides in your head or on your heart.

Family members can wreck a nerve, especially when they haven't given their lives over to Christ. But it can be equally difficult dealing with those who have accepted him as their Lord and Savior but refuse to come to church on a regular basis. My experience has taught me that talking Christian principles to some people is like speaking in a foreign language. I don't mean to be disrespectful, but the Bible does say, "Do not cast your precious pearls before a swine." Our wanting to assist our loved ones becomes a heavy burden, because we know what Jesus could do for them if they would only open up their hearts and minds to his love and his teachings.

Family members aren't the only ones who can apply some unmerited pressures and burdens on our lives. Friends and coworkers can get underneath our skin as well. There are some friends and coworkers who have studied us and watched us over the years, and when they are in a bad mood, they know exactly how to get us in a bad mood, too. Over a period of time, you share intimate things with them about you and your family, and they are able to manipulate your mind by playing on your sensibilities, saying what they would do if your situation were happening to their family or on their job. And because we are looking for somebody to help bear the burden of what's going on, we listen to them, even when the advice is not sound. And then we find ourselves in a more frustrating situation than we were in prior to even discussing the situation with them!

Brothers, this is why we need to be careful about whom we talk to about our situations, and be even more careful about from whom we take advice regarding our situations. You do remember when Jesus had to rebuke Peter for some advice Peter attempted to give him about not dying on the cross. This is why we need to have a relationship with God for ourselves and to have a person in our lives who has a healthy and ongoing relationship with the Father, the Son, and the Holy Ghost!

You need to surround yourself with someone who has a direct prayer line to the Lord, somebody who knows how to get on their knees to pray not only for their own salvation, but for your salvation as well. You need to be around somebody who can tell you what the Lord says. You need to be around somebody who can tell you how they got over the rough sides of the mountain. You need to be around somebody who spends time in Sunday school and who does not mind investing in a study Bible and concordance. You need to be around somebody who, like Paul, is not ashamed of the Gospel of Jesus the Christ. You need to be around somebody who will say a positive thing about the Lord, and not a negative thing about your life. You need to be around somebody who understands that a true friend is somebody who will get in your way when they see you going down. You need to be around somebody who will rejoice in the name of the Lord when they see you growing in the Lord and see the Lord growing in you!

Yes, family members, friends, and coworkers can place some tremendous burdens upon your bending back! This is a burden that all men of God must bear, just as Moses did in the text. My black brothers who are in the church, and those who are not in the church, you must remember that God can forgive you for any and all of the sins of your past. The Bible says, "If we confess our sins, he who is faithful and just will forgive us our sins and cleanse us from all unrighteousness. If we say that we have not sinned, we make him a liar, and his word is not in us" (1 John 1: 9–10). The things that you have done or said in the past that have kept you from reaching your destiny can be cleansed from your soul if you would give them to the Burden Bearer. Strangers, colleagues, and relatives will attempt to take your joy, but the world can't take from you what it didn't give you. The joy that ought to be perched upon your soul should be from the Burden Bearer. Don't allow society—not even your fellow brothers—to keep you from worshiping God in truth and in spirit.

Any and all sanctified believers will admit that it is hard living an authentic Christian life. But we as African American men must do our very best to model the life of Jesus. It was the church folk who crucified Jesus; therefore, we as authentic Christian men must sustain our rules within the church, as well as outside the confines of the church walls.

Living in America as a black man, let alone a Christian black man, is full of challenges. The standard of a man, the ethos of a community, has been set forth by an establishment that has systematically set roadblocks and glass ceilings in the paths of African American men. Yet the burdens of providing for and protecting our families remain the same. The larger society expects black men to be able to compete with everyone, but the opportunities are not truly available. There is no question, my brothers, that black men possess the skills, the fortitude, and the ability to achieve, but there are highly sophisticated barriers in place in all facets of our lives that are designed to block our success. The school system is not designed for our children's education but for their "miseducation," as was noted by the renowned scholar Carter G. Woodson over five decades ago. The penal system, which is a perennial revolving door, is not designed for our reformation, but for our annihilation as African American men. Black men are still the last hired and the first fired, primarily due to the social injustices that run rampant in the larger community. Accordingly, we are not just unemployed, we are underemployed and underpaid, which creates additional burdens—manmade burdens—that few others have to contend with.

Despite all of the social ills and limited earthly resources facing black men in particular, we as Christian men are expected to overcome, to remain steadfast and faithful. Why? Because God has fashioned men to be able to do it, God expects us to do it, and our women and children need us to do it.

With so many earthly burdens facing us as black men, I'd like to raise a relevant question that all of us must consider: "Who do you go to in order to relieve your burdens?" In other words, who do you go to for counsel in the midnight hour? Who do you go to when your bills are overdue? Who do you go to when your kids have gone astray? Who do you go to when your friends won't return your calls? Who do you go to when you can't get your spouse to act right, or when you aren't acting right with your spouse? Who do you got to when the painkillers, and even the doctors, don't or can't relieve your pain? Who do you go to when there appear to be more dark days and dreary nights than sunrises and sunsets?

These are the questions African American men must deal with in their personal lives and in their public lives. So I want to talk about where black men must go to get assistance for the burdens that others place upon them. Let me tell you about the only place that we can go. The only place that we can go is to the Burden Bearer, because he says that no weapon formed against his anointed shall prosper. We as African American men know the Burden Bearer as Zion's leaning post. We as African American men know the Burden Bearer as the lily of the valley. We as African American men know the Burden Bearer as a presence in times of trouble. We as African American men know the Burden Bearer as the bishop of all souls, living and dead.

Our grandfathers know the Burden Bearer as their walking cane. Blind folks know the Burden Bearer as the light in the midst of their darkness. Hungry folks know the Burden Bearer as the bread in the midst of their hunger. Moses knew the Burden Bearer as the God of Abraham, Isaac, and Jacob. And we in the church know the Burden Bearer as Jesus the Christ. There are some burdens that we cannot carry with our physical strength, so we must turn them over to Jesus. Jesus directs us to come unto him, to learn of him, and to cast our burdens upon him because his yoke is easy and his burden is light.

Can I tell you why he's the one you need to go to, my brethren? The text shows us three reasons we need to go to the Lord for relief from our burdens. First and foremost, you want to go to the Lord because the Lord knows you. Brothers, the Burden Bearer knows things about you that you don't even know about yourself. He knows what makes you happy and what makes you sad. He knows what makes you laugh and what makes you cry. He knows what lifts you up and what brings you down. He knows what will make you strong and what will make you weak. Brothers, the Burden Bearer knows when your smile is there only to cover up your frown. God knows when your laughter is there only to prevent you from crying. God knows what you are thinking even when you aren't saying anything. God knows when the pain is becoming unbearable. He is a God who can't be fooled, for he is a discerner of the thoughts and the intentions of your heart. For the Bible says that man looks at the outward appearance, but God looks at the inward appearance. This may be why we don't take our burdens to the Lord, because he knows us so well that we can't bully him like we do our friends, family, coworkers, and even our pastor. We can tell others a story in such a way that pity, empathy, sympathy, and compassion can steer the advice that they give to accommodate us. But God knows the advice that's good for us; God is not going to allow us to intimidate him.

Moses is displeased, so says Numbers 11:10. Moses wants to make it seem like the situation is brought forth because of his position. But the truth is, Moses is displeased at the decisions that God has made for God's people. And instead of being man enough to say to God that he is mad at God, Moses wants to blame it on other things and other people. Black men, you can tell God your true feelings because he already knows your feelings, and he is a God who is big enough to handle you and your feelings. For the Word says that he has our names written on the palm of his hand, and that his hand is so large that it can measure the heavens with just the span of two. Surely, if his hand can do this, then his hand can also mold you to be who it is that he will have you to be. And his hand can embrace you in a manner in which, even in your frustration, you can still sing the great Baptist song, "Hold onto His hands, God's Unchanging Hands." The Bible says that the Lord is like an eagle that watches over her brood. He knows you.

Secondly, the text shows us that the Lord knows your problem. In Numbers 10:11–15, Moses gives a litany of his perceived problems. He says that the Lord has afflicted him. He says that he has not found favor in the Lord's sight. He says that the Lord has laid the burden of the people upon him. He says that it is his job to find the flesh that the people desire to eat. Then, he shows a little bit of honesty and says that he is not able to bear all of the people's burdens.

Now the interesting note about this is that Moses is focusing on his perceived problems as opposed to concentrating on God's potential display of power and might. Moses is doing what a lot of us as African American men do today: He is being self-centered, focusing on his problems and not on God's power. Moses is now required to trust God a little more than he has had to do in the past. He is allowing the cries of the people to weigh heavily on his heart, and he is taking personal responsibility for the well-being of the people as opposed to keeping in mind that the people aren't his, but God's. And the problems are not his, but God's. Moses is becoming too attached to the people's personal problems and is not allowing God to direct his path. Therefore, Moses feels that he has a problem, but his problem is not to provide all of the wants and desires of the people. His problem now is in continuing to trust God to do through him for the people.

Moses is beginning to act like he is God. Many black men today possess a "messiah complex" just like Moses did. We believe that things can't get done unless we do it. We believe that if we don't accommodate our wives like they want to be accommodated, then we aren't good mates. We believe that if we don't buy our children all of the things they request, then we aren't good providers. Brothers, you can't let folks put you in the grave before God is ready. You can't let folks pressure you into being what they want you to be. You are a being made of flesh, and you are limited in all that you can do; only God is omnipotent! You can't be in all places at all times; only God is omnipresent! You can't know the answers to all your members' problems; only God is omniscient! And the saddest reality is that you can't save anybody; only God, through his son Jesus Christ, possesses salvific power. God, the Burden Bearer, knows your limitations, even as his prophet, priest, shepherd, and servant. He has given us things to help us to do his will, if we would only listen to his words, for the Bible says that "heaven and earth will pass away, but [God's] words will not pass away" (Luke 21:33). And this leads me to my third point.

The third point is that the Lord knows your answer. God tells Moses to stop complaining and to get seventy elders of the congregation and bring them down to the tabernacle. And God goes on to say, "When you bring them to the tabernacle, Moses, I am going to take your spirit and put it on the seventy elders so that they can help to alleviate some of the stress, anxiety, pressure, confusion, static, and burdens that are on you as a man of God, serving in the Wilderness Missionary Baptist Church of Israel. I do this because I am the Burden Bearer." Essentially, what God does is to give Moses what I call the "Courage of Self-Evaluation Theology."

This theology requires you, African American men, to look at the God who is in you prior to looking at the God in someone else. This theology requires you to administer a spiritual inventory of yourself prior to attempting to discern the spiritual formation of someone else. This theology demands that you assess your weaknesses and strengths before casting opinions about people around you. This theology mandates that you inspect the possible flaws within your own spiritual maturity before analyzing the people who may be causing the anxiety in your life. Simply put, you must have your own house in order prior to attempting to assist people with the affairs of their house.

The Burden Bearer shows Moses that there are people besides Moses who can help in changing a community, and that the only thing Moses needs to do is to allow the Burden Bearer to raise people of like spirits in Moses' inner circle. We as African American men need to be asking God for help in all of our affairs. The Bible says that we must acknowledge God in all of our doings. The Burden Bearer knows the answer to all of your problems. My brothers, he knows the intentions of your heart. He knows when you need a friend. He knows what you need for your family. He knows when you need to be raised or lowered. He knows when you need to be scolded or forgiven. He knows when you are ready to assume new and greater responsibilities.

In fact, the Bible says, in 2 Chronicles 7:14, "If my people who are called by my name humble themselves, pray, seek my face, and turn from their wicked ways, then will I hear from heaven, and will forgive their sin and heal their land." Black men, God has the answers to our problems. David says in Psalm 40:1–4,

I waited patiently for the LORD; he inclined to me and heard my cry. He drew me up from the desolate pit, out of the miry bog, and set my feet upon a rock, making my steps secure. He put a new song in my mouth, a song of praise to our God. Many will see and fear, and put their trust in the LORD. Happy are those who make the LORD their trust, who do not turn to the proud, to those who go astray after false gods.

Brothers, turn your life over to God, the Burden Bearer.

about the contributors

Dr. Claude R. Alexander Jr. is pastor of University Park Baptist Church in Charlotte, North Carolina. During his ten years there, the church has grown from a congregation of fewer than five hundred members to more than six thousand. Dr. Alexander was morning worship leader at the 1999 Hampton University Ministers' Conference Choir Directors' Organists' Guild Workshop. His civic involvements include chairing the board of directors of the Charlotte Mecklenburg Urban League.

Dr. Charles E. Booth has served since 1978 as pastor of Mt. Olivet Baptist Church in Columbus, Ohio. He is also professor of preaching at Trinity Lutheran Seminary in Columbus. In 1993 Dr. Booth was listed in *Ebony* magazine's Honor Roll of Great Preachers.

Rev. Timothy J. Clarke is pastor of First Church of God in Columbus, Ohio, and bishop in the Church of God (Anderson, Indiana). He also serves the church at large as an evangelist and teacher. He is the author of three books: *Signs of His Coming, Signs of the Times,* and *Help for Those Who Hurt.*

Dr. Otis Moss Jr. is pastor of Olivet Institutional Baptist Church in Cleveland, Ohio. He was called to the ministry at the age of seventeen, during his days as a student at Morehouse College in Atlanta, Georgia. He now serves Morehouse as chair of the Board of Trustees.

Rev. Otis Moss III has served as pastor of the historic Tabernacle Baptist Church in Augusta, Georgia, since 1997. While a master of divinity student at Yale University, he was awarded the FTE

Benjamin Elijah Mays Scholarship in Religion and the Yale University Magee Fellowship. *Newsweek* magazine recently cited Rev. Moss as one of "God's foot soldiers," committed to transforming the lives of youth.

Rev. James C. Perkins is pastor of Greater Christ Baptist Church in Detroit, Michigan, and founder of the Benjamin E. Mays Male Academy. He is the author of the Judson Press book *Building Up Zion's Walls* and has also contributed to *Outstanding Black Sermons, Volume 4* and to both volumes of *From One Brother to Another.*

Rev. Darryl D. Sims is pastor at Shiloh Baptist Church in Massillon, Ohio. He is also the founder and president of DLR Learning Center, which focuses on improving the quality of life for African-American youth, particularly males. In addition to serving as editor for this volume, he is founder and president of Evangucation Ministries, which combines "evangelism" and "education" to improve the spiritual formation and educational development of African Americans.

Dr. Walter S. Thomas is pastor of the New Psalmist Baptist Church in Baltimore, Maryland. He is the author of two Judson Press books: *Spiritual Navigation for the 21st Century* and *Good Meat Makes Its Own Gravy.* He served as president of the 2000 Hampton University Ministers' Conference Choir Directors' Organists' Guild Workshop

Dr. Donald J. Washington is pastor of the Mt. Hermon Missionary Baptist Church in Columbus, Ohio. He is the immediate past president of The Ohio Baptist General Convention and Auxiliaries, Inc. A Vietnam War veteran, he was called to full-time ministry in 1983.

Rev. Ralph Douglas West is founder and senior pastor of Brookhollow Baptist Church (also known as The Church Without Walls) in Houston, Texas. The church began in 1987 with thirty-two people meeting in Rev. West's home. The average weekly attendance today is 4,800.

Dr. C. Dexter Wise is pastor of Faith Ministries Interdenominational Church in Columbus, Ohio. He grew up in Baltimore, Maryland, was licensed to preach at age sixteen, and ordained to the gospel ministry at age nineteen. In 1991 he was called to organize the church he currently pastors. He has written several books and produced two rap albums. During a fifty-school tour over ninety days, the "rappin' Reverend" got more than eighteen thousand schoolchildren in Columbus, Ohio, to make public commitments to live drug-free, crime-free and alcohol-free lives.

Dr. Jeremiah A. Wright Jr. is senior pastor of Trinity United Church of Christ in Chicago, Illinois. A gifted musician, he wrote and composed "Jesus Is His Name" and "God Will Answer Prayer," both of which were recorded by the Trinity Choral Ensemble on their Trinity label. Dr. Wright is the author of four books, including the Judson Press titles *Good News!* and *What Makes You So Strong?* He is also the editor of the Judson Press devotional *From One Brother to Another, Volume II.*